**THIS IS A BORZOI BOOK
PUBLISHED BY
ALFRED A. KNOPF, INC**

Copyright © 1998 Alfred A.
Knopf Inc., New York

ISBN 0-375-70256-3

Library of Congress number
97-80570

*First published May 1998
Revised and updated Feb. 1999*

Originally published in France
by Nouveaux Loisirs, a
subsidiary of Gallimard, Paris
1997, and in Italy by Touring
Editore, Srl., Milano 1997.
Copyright © 1997
Nouveaux Loisirs,
Touring Editore, Srl.

SERIES EDITORS
Seymourina Cruse, Marisa Bassi
MILAN EDITION:
Mélani Le Bris, Caroline
Cuny, Seymourina Cruse
SECOND EDITION:
Amandine Galopin,
Marina Forlizzi
GRAPHICS
Élizabeth Cohat, Yann Le Duc
LAYOUT (MILAN):
Silvia Pecora
AIRPORT MAPS
Kristoff Chemineau
MINI-MAPS
Studio Wise
AROUND MILAN MAPS:
Édigraphie
STREET MAPS:
Touring Club Italiano
PRODUCTION
Catherine Bourrabier

Translated by Ruth
Blackmore

Edited and typeset by Book
Creation Services, London

Printed in Italy by
Editoriale Lloyd

Authors
MILAN

Things you need to know:
Roberto Franzoni (1)
Roberto Franzoni is an architect and a
journalist and also used to be a navigator
and pilot. He has traveled widely and lived
in a number of places, from Liguria to the
Caribbean, and now lives in Milan. He
is the former editor of the magazine
Uomo Mare Vogue.

Where to stay and
Where to eat Piero Bolfo (2)
Piero Bolfo has managed several top
establishments, from the Passo Penice
Hotel to Canoviano (a restaurant in the
center of Milan). He has been President
of the Unione Restoranti del Buon Ricordo
since 1972 and oversaw the publication of
the food and catering directories, *Il Codice
della Cucina Italiana* and *Ristorazione
Professionale Italiana.*

After dark: Carlo Montanaro (3)
Carlo Montanaro has lived in Milan for
40 years and has been in journalism for
20. After covering the big racing and sailing
events for the *Gazzetta dello Sport*, he
became assistant editor of the magazine
Auto in Vogue and of the monthly *Dove*.
He later launched *Carnet*, a magazine on
leisure pursuits.

What to see and
Further afield: Gianni Bagioli (4)
Gianni Bagioli, born in Bergamo, lives in
Milan and works in publishing and tourism.
He has been coordinator of the Touring
Club's guides to Italy and consultant editor
since the 1960s..

Where to shop:
Monica Bogliardi (5)
Monica Bogliardi, born in Milan, has a
degree in philosophy and specialized in
esthetics. In 1990 after attending the
School of Journalism in Milan, she started
writing columns on fashion, consumerism
and society for the magazine *Panorama.*

Things you need to know ➡ 6

Where to stay ➡ 16

Where to eat ➡ 42

After dark ➡ 72

What to see ➡ 84

Further afield ➡ 102

Where to shop ➡ 118

Maps ➡ 146

Symbols

- ☎ telephone
- ➡ fax
- ● price or price range
- 🕐 opening hours
- ▣ credit cards accepted
- ▣ credit cards not accepted
- 📞 toll-free number
- @ e-mail address
- ★ hot tips and advice

Access

- Ⓜ nearest subway(s)
- 🚌 bus (or tram)
- 🅿 private parking lot
- 🚘 valet parking
- ♿ no facilities for the disabled
- 🚆 train
- 🚗 car
- ⛴ boat

Hotels

- ☎ telephone in room
- 📠 fax in room on request
- 🍸 mini-bar in room
- 📺 television in room
- ❄ air conditioning in room
- 🕐 24-hour room service
- 🛎 porter
- 👶 child-minding, babysitting
- ✉ meeting room(s)
- 🚫 no pets
- 🍳 breakfast
- ☕ afternoon tea
- 🍴 restaurant on site
- 🎵 live music
- 🌙 nightclub
- 🌳 garden, patio or terrace
- 🏋 gym, health club
- 🏊 swimming pool, sauna

Restaurants

- 🥗 vegetarian dishes
- 🏞 outstanding views
- 👔 smart dress required
- 🚬 smoking section(s)
- 🍸 bar area

Sightseeing

- 🎁 gift stores
- 🚩 guided tours
- ☕ cafeteria

Stores

- 🏬 branches, outlets

The Insider's Guide is made up of **8 sections** each indicated by a different color.

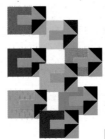

Things you need to know (mauve);
Where to stay (blue);
Where to eat (red);
After dark (pink);
What to see (green);
Further afield (orange);
Where to shop (yellow);
Finding your way (purple).

Practical information is given for each particular establishment: opening times, prices, ways of paying, different services available.

"Budget!"
This star symbol highlights low-cost hotels and restaurants.

How to use this guide

In the area
Brera was once the 'artists' quarter'. Young a
their meal with their latest canvas. Today this
been replaced by attractive boutiques, antiqu

at to see
■ Where to
134

37
38

Piazza Foro

M *Lan*

The section
"In the area"
refers you (➡ 00) to
other establishments
that are covered in a
different section of the
guide but found in the
same area of the city.

Brera (Lanza) **A** A1 - B2

42 16 47

M *Lanza* Via Pontaccio
45 ⑫ ⑮ 11
46 ⑯ V. Fiori Chiari V. Fiori
43 44
28
47 44

The small map
shows all the
establishments mentioned
and others described
elsewhere but found "in
the area", by the color of
the section.

**The name of the
district** is given above
the map. A grid
reference (**A** A1-B2)
enables you to find it in
the section on Maps at
the end of the book.

with the seasons ★ : spring salad
all… All diners are treated to an

Hot tips, indicated by a star ★, contains advice
from the author: the best rooms, recommended
dishes, view not to be missed.

Not forgetting
■ **Orient Express (15)** via Fior
Relive, in the heart of Brera, the atmos

The section "Not forgetting"
lists other useful addresses in the same area.

The opening page
to each section contains
an index ordered
alphabetically (Getting
there), but subject or by
district (After dark) as
well as useful addresses
and advice.

**The section
"Things you need
to know"**
covers information

on getting to Milan
and day-to-day life in
the city.

Theme pages
focus on a particular
topic.

The maps section of
this guide, entitled
"Finding your way",
contains a street index,
a metro map and 9
detailed maps.

Getting there

Finding the number

The Italian equivalent of our Yellow Pages, the *Pagine Gialle*, can be found in all pay phones. You can also access *Pagine Gialle* on the internet @ *www.paginegialle.it*. For international directory enquiries: ☎ 176 Various tourist brochures also contain useful telephone numbers.

Changing money

Banks and bureaux de change licensed by the Bank of Italy give the best rate of exchange. Hotels, private bureaux de change and those at stations are likely to charge a high commission, but are open outside normal banking hours.

Formalities, passports and visas

EU nationals can enter and stay in Italy as long as they wish provide
they have a valid passport. Citizens from the US, Canada, Australia an
New Zealand can stay in Italy for up to three months provided they
have a valid passport. This can be extended by obtaining a special visa in
advance from an Italian embassy or consulate.

42 Things you need to know

Internet

Internet cafés are becoming more
and more popular in Italy. This is
one that we can recommend:
Hard Disk Café, *corso Sempione 44*
☎ *02331 01038* @ *www.hdc.it*
🕐 *Mon.–Sat. 7am–2pm.*

Motorists

Motorists need a driving license and
insurance papers. They should obtain
a Green Card from their insurers
proving that they are covered by
third-party insurance. Non-EU
citizens should ideally have an
international driving license with an
Italian translation incorporated.

Consulates and embassies in Milan

Australia: *via Borgogna 2* ☎ *02777041*
Canada: *via Vittorio Pisani 19* ☎ *0267581*
UK: *via San Paolo 7* ☎ *028693442*
USA: *via Principe Amedeo 2/10* ☎ *0290351*

...by two airports: Linate Airport and Malpensa Airport. ...side the city; Malpensa, which is planned to handle ...ternational flights, is about 30 miles from Milan in ...of Lake Maggiore.

Getting there

Linate

Information
☎ 0274852200
🕐 daily
7am–11pm
Recorded information
Domestic arrivals
☎ 0228106282
International arrivals
☎ 0228106310
Domestic departures
☎ 0228106300
International departures
☎ 0228106324
Lost Luggage
☎ 0270124451

Buses
No. 73
The no. 73 bus runs between the airport and the city center. The terminus is piazza San Babila. Tickets are the same as those used on the city's public transportation.
🕐 daily 6am–1am departures every 20 mins. Journey time: 20 mins

Stam bus
The Stam bus shuttles between the airport and Stazione Centrale. The terminus is piazza Luigi Savoia
☎ 0266984509
🕐 daily 5.40am–9pm; departures every 20 mins approx. Journey time: 25 mins.
● 4500 lire

Taxis
From the airport to the center: 30 mins
● 30,000 lire

Car rental
Avis
☎ 02717214
🕐 daily 7.30am–midnight
Hertz
☎ 0270200256
🕐 daily 7.30am–12.30am

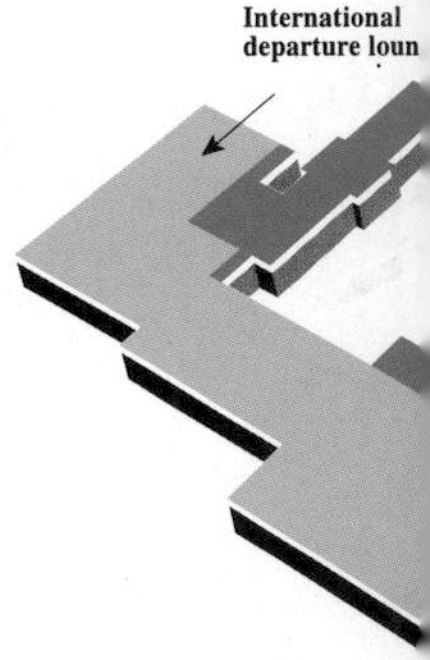

International departure loun...

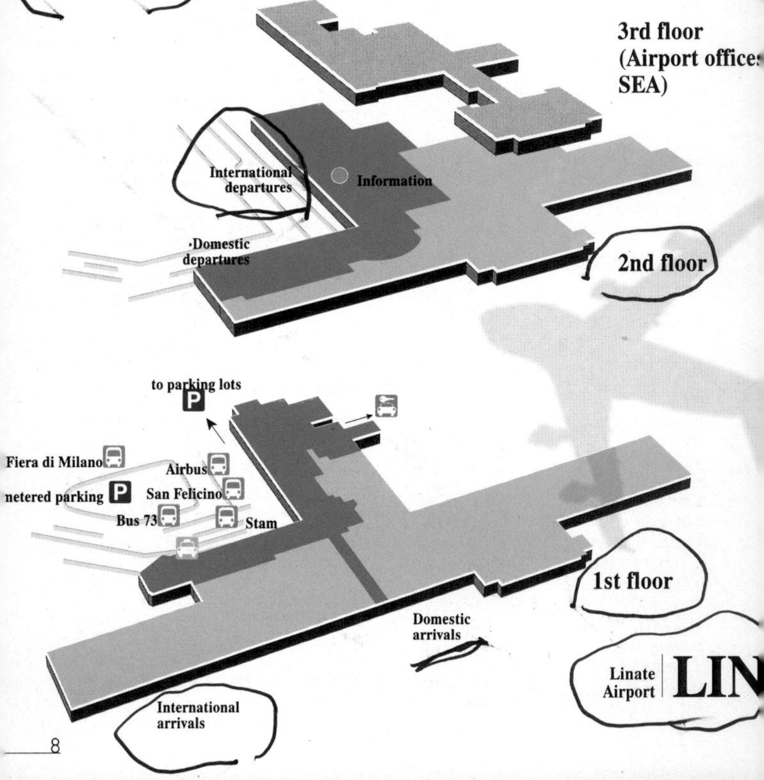

3rd floor
(Airport offices SEA)

International departures

Information

Domestic departures

2nd floor

to parking lots
P

Fiera di Milano

Airbus

metered parking P
San Felicino

Bus 73

Stam

1st floor

Domestic arrivals

International arrivals

Linate Airport | LIN...

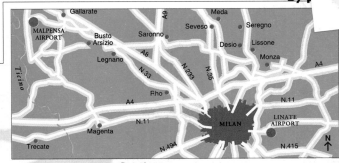

Domestic
departure lounge

International
arrivals

Departures

Arrivals

Domestic
arrivals

Arona Gallarate
Information

Car rental

Connecting bus to Linate

Gallarate FFSS Linea Zappa

Milano Stazione Centrale
and Lampugnano

Airbus
(tickets for
Milan and Linate)

Airline
company
buses

P

Malpensa
Intercontinental Airport | **MXP**

Alitalia
Milan ☎ 02147865642
UK ☎ 0171-602 7111
US ☎ (212) 582 8900
British Airways
Milan ☎ 02809892
UK ☎ 0345-222111
US ☎ 1-800 247 9297

P Parking

Taxis

Buses

Car rental

Post office
☎ 02717847

Assistance
☎ 0274852223

Hotel
Novotel Milano
Est Aeroporto
via Mecenate 121
➔ 02580 11085
➔ 02580 11086
Connections
between
Malpensa and
Linate airports
Information
☎ 0240099260
☎ 0240099280
Journey time:
75 mins.
● 18,000 lire

Malpensa

Information
☎ 0274852200
🕐 daily 7am–11pm
Domestic arrivals
☎ 0226800463
International
arrivals
☎ 0226800619
Domestic
departures
☎ 02268 00606
International
departures
☎ 02268 00627

Lost luggage
🕐 The office is
open daily 7am–
11pm
☎ 0274854215

Buses
Malpensa
Shuttle
Terminates at
Stazione Centrale
or piazza Castello,
with one stop at
Fiera di Milano.
Journey time: 1 hr
☎ 0240099260
or 0240099280
● 13,000 lire

Connections to
Linate airport
Information:
☎ 0240099260
or 0240099280
Journey: 75 mins

Taxis
The taxi rank is at
the exit of the
terminal.
From the airport to
the center: approx.

1 hr ● approx.
130,000 lire

Car rental
In the airport:
Avis
☎ 0240099375
🕐 daily 7.30am–
9pm
Eurodollar
☎ 0240099737
🕐 8am–8pm
Hertz
☎ 0240099000
🕐 7.30am–8pm

Post office
☎ 0240099332

Assistance
☎ 0274854444

Hotel
Hotel Oleggio
via Verbano 19
☎ 032193301
➔ 032193377

The Stazione Centrale (1), connected to the center of Milan by two metro lines (2), is northern Italy's biggest and busiest railroad junction. The arrivals/departures hall (3) has a tourist information office (4), stores (5), and a ticket office (6). The Pendolino (7), the high-speed train run by

Getting there

By train

The numbers in brackets refer to the small inset map.

[1] Stazione Centrale
The main station is connected to the center by the metro lines M2 and M3 (green and yellow).
Tickets
You can buy tickets at the station and in travel bureaux. The Ferrovie dello Stato runs a telephone booking service; you can book a ticket up to 24 hours before departure.
☎ 0266981013

🕙 *daily 8am–8pm (Sat., Sun. reservations only).*
Information
☎ 147888088
🕙 *daily 7am–9pm*
Schedules and connections
☎ 02166105050
🕙 *daily 24 hours*
Arrivals (recorded information)
☎ 0266984615
Lost property
☎ 0263712667
🕙 *daily 7am–1pm, 2–8pm*
Left luggage
Galleria Partenze
☎ 0263712212
🕙 *daily 24 hrs*
Disabled travelers
Assistance
☎ 0267070958

Car rental
Avis
☎ 026690280
🕙 *Mon.–Fri. 7.45am–9pm; Sat. 8am–4pm; Sun. 8am–1pm*
Europcar
☎ 0266981589
🕙 *Mon.–Fri. 8am–4pm, Sat. 8.30am–1pm*
Hertz
☎ 026690061
🕙 *Mon.–Fri. 8am–7pm, Sat. 8am–2pm*
Maggiore Budget
☎ 026690934
🕙 *Mon.–Fri. 8am–1pm, 2–7.30pm; Sat. 8.30am–12.30pm, 3–7pm*
[2] Stazione Garibaldi
Stazione Garibaldi

is connected to the center by metro line M2 (green).
Information
☎ 026552078
🕙 *daily 6am–10pm*
Tickets
☎ 0265592491
Lost property
☎ 026376110
[3] Stazione Lambrate
The station, in the Città Studi area, is connected to the center by metro line M2 (green).
[4] Stazione delle Ferrovie Nord Milano
The station is connected to the center by metro line M1 (red). The Ferrovie

the Ferrovie dello Stato (the state railroad company) (8) stops here. Motorists with a Viacard (9) ➡ 11 will have fewer delays getting through the tolls.

Nord network runs trains to Brianza, Como and Varese.
Information
☎ 0248066771
🕐 24 hours
Lost property
☎ 028511559
🕐 daily 8am–noon, 1.30-4.30pm
[5] Stazione Porta Genova
The station is connected to the center by metro line M2 (green). Trains leave here for Vigevano, Mortara and Alessandria (Piedmont).
Tickets
☎ 0258100143
🕐 daily 6.30am–8.30pm

By car
Milan is encircled by a number of *tangenziali* (ring roads), which are connected to the highways and roads into the city center. There are frequent traffic jams on roads coming into and going out of the city during rush hour. Some roads have tolls.
Highways
A1
The A1, known as the 'sunshine highway' (Autostrada del Sole), runs from Milan to Rome via the cities of Bologna and Florence.

A4
The A4 runs across the north of Italy from Turin to Venice. The section that goes through Bergamo, Brescia and other major towns in the Veneto is called the 'Serenissima' route (Autostrada Serenissima).
A7
The A7, known as the 'highway of flowers' (Autostrada dei Fiori), is the main route down to Genoa.
A8–A9
This route, called the 'Milan-Lakes' highway

(Autostrada dei Laghi), takes you to Varese. The A9 section goes to Como and Switzerland via the Chiasso pass.
Viacard
This pre-payment card reduces your waiting time at tolls. It's sold at service stations and toll-booths.
Speed limits
In Italy the speed limit is 80mph on highways, 55mph on secondary roads and 30mph in built-up areas.
Road organizations
Automobile Club of Italy (ACI)
☎ 116

Basic facts

The subway network in Milan has only three lines, but is fast and efficient. The city also has trams (1), buses (2) and trolleybuses. Below: a bus stop and a some ATM tickets (3); a subway sign (4); a metro stop on the yellow line (5); a street sign in one of the city's cobbled streets (6); a parking sign (7); a Sosta-

Getting around

Subway

The metropolitana is Milan's fastest form of public transport. Subway signs are red with a white letter M.

Schedules

The subway runs from 6am to around midnight. After midnight a bus service takes over and runs along the same route as the red line (M1) between Sesto F.S. and Molino Dorino.

Getting around on the subway

There are three lines: the M1 (red line), which crosses the city from east to west; the M2 (green line), which connects the main railroad stations; and the M3 (yellow line), which runs from north to south.

Information

Duomo subway station
🕐 *Mon.–Sat. 7.30am–7.30pm*
☎ *0248032403*
Stazione Centrale subway station
🕐 *Mon.–Sat. 8am–7.45pm*
☎ *026697032*

Passante Ferroviaro

This railway network links the northwest of the city with the three subway lines. Trains run into the city from 6.40am to 8.10pm and out of the city from 6.55am to 8.25pm.

Trams, buses, trolleybuses

Trams, buses and trolleybuses are run by the Milan transport authority (ATM). They run from between 4am and 6am until between midnight and 1am.

Getting around on ATM transport

All stops are marked by signs showing the route, connections and schedules. You will need to signal to the driver as all stops are request stops.

Tickets

Tickets for travel in the city center cost a flat fee of 1500 lire. When you get on, you have to punch your ticket in the machines on board. The ticket is then valid for 75 mins for several trips on buses or trams or for one trip on the subway. Tickets cannot be bought on board; you have to buy them in advance from a tobacconist's, a news-stand, a bar or a ticket machine near one of the main stops. Tickets for travel in the city center are valid as far as Sesto Marelli (M1) and Cascina Gobba (M2). To travel further out of

milano travel card (8); taxis in Milan are either white or yellow (9).

the city you need a different ticket (*extraurbano*).

Travel passes

You can buy a special pass costing 6000 lire which gives you 24 hours unlimited travel (from the first time you punch it) on buses, trams and the subway. You can also get a 48-hour pass for 9000 lire.

Weekly travelcard

This card costs 20,000 lire (you will need a passport photo) and is valid from Monday to Sunday on all public transport systems.

Taxis

You can phone for a taxi:
Radiotaxi
☎ 026767
☎ 028585
☎ 028388
☎ 025251

Charges

Taxis are fairly expensive in Milan. The average meter starts at 600 lire. There are extra charges for baggage and late-night travel.

Cars

There is a lot of traffic in Milan, but it is less chaotic than in other Italian cities. Note that parking places are rarely free. The historic center (*zona A*) is divided into five districts identified by five distinct colors (see map above). To go from one district to another you have to follow the ring road and use the one-way system to get back into the center.

Parking

Parking is restricted in the center: you can park in the zones marked with blue lines if you have a *Sostamilano* card. Parking on roadsides marked with yellow lines is for residents only. There are many underground parking lots, though these are more expensive than those above

ground.

Where to buy Sostamilano

At tobacconists', news-stands, and some bars.

Schedules/charges

From 8am to 8pm parking in zones marked with blue lines costs 2500 lire an hour, limited to two hours maximum. Between 8pm and midnight there is a flate rate of 5000 lire for any length of stay up to four hours.

ATM parking lots

These are a good alternative. There are about 12 on the outskirts near the subway stops or the termini.

13

Basic facts

The Milan tourist board (APT) (1) is a helpful and reliable source of information about many aspects of the the city. Below: phone booth (2); telephone card (3); central post office (4); post office sign (5); stamps (6); mail box (7); Bancomat credit card and Italian currency (8); exchange

Getting by

OMNIAPRESS

agenzia ANSA

TUTTOMAGLIA

adnkronos

Avanti!

STAMPA SERA

Il Messaggero

LA STAMPA

TUTTOSPORT

POSTE

CHANGE·EXCHANGE
CAMBIO·WECHSEL

9

10

8

BANCOMAT

PRELEVAMENTI
E PAGAMENTI
AUTOMATICI IN ITALIA

PRELEVAMENTI
AUTOMATICI
ALL'ESTERO

1

2

8

Media

The numbers in brackets refer to the small inset map.

The Italian press

The nine major national dailies are: Il Corriere della Sera; La Repubblica; Il Sole 24 Ore; La Gazzetta dello Sport; Il Giornale; L'Unità; La Stampa. Good weekly supplements come with the Wednesday edition of Il Corriere della Sera (Vivi Milano) and the Thursday edition of La Repubblica (Tutto Milano).

International press

The news-stands in the center

(especially in piazza del Duomo and piazza della Scala) sell international newspapers. Same-day papers usually arrive by noon.

Radio

There are three national radio stations (RAI) and several private stations.

Television

There are three RAI (public) channels and three Mediaset channels (Canale 5, Italia 1 and Rete 4).

Money

Currency

The currency is the Italian lira (abbreviated to LIT). Bank notes come in denominations

from 1000 to 500,000 lire, and coins from 50 to 1000 lire.

Banks

You can withdraw cash from banks.
☽ *Mon.–Fri. 8.30am–1.30pm, 2.45–3.45pm*

Bureaux de change

Cit
Galleria Vittorio Emanuele II
☎ *02863701*
☽ *Mon.–Fri. 9am–7pm;*
Sat. 9am–1pm, 2–6pm

Exact
Stazione Centrale, Galleria Partenze
Accepts traveler's checks.
☎ *0266984797*
☽ *7am–10.30pm*

Punto Duomo
via Orefici 2
Accepts traveler's checks.

☎ *0286464178*
☽ *9am–9pm*

Credit cards

Paying by credit card or using it to withdraw cash is very common in Italy. Automatic tellers (Bancomats) at banks will give you money if you have a PIN number. Numbers to phone if your cards are lost or stolen:

Visa-Mastercard
☎ *167821001-3*
American Express
☎ *0672282*

Tips

Add at least 10% extra to the total of any bill.

Telephone

Dialing codes

To call Milan from the rest of Italy, dial 02 then the 7- or 8-digit

rates (9); advertisement signs for a variety of Italian newspapers and press agencies in Milan.

number. To call Milan from the USA and Canada first dial 011 followed by 39 (for Italy) followed by 02 (the Milan code); from the UK and Ireland first dial 00 39 02; from Australia dial 0011 39 02; from New Zealand dial 00 44 39 02. To call abroad from Italy, dial the international prefix (for the USA and Canada 001, for the UK 0044, for Ireland 00353, for Australia 0061, for New Zealand 0064) then dial the number you require. **International directory enquiries** ☎ 176

Collect calls ☎ 170
Telecom offices *Galleria Vittorio Emanuele II* 🕐 8.30am–9.30pm *Stazione Centrale* 🕐 8am–8pm
Public pay phones Public phones take coins, tokens (*gettone*) or phonecards.

Post offices

Area post offices 🕐 Mon.–Fri. 8.30am–1.50pm; Sat. 8.30am–noon; last day of the month 8.30–11.40am
[6] Main post office *via Cordusio 4/ piazza Edison* ☎ 02869 2136

Registered mail 🕐 Mon.–Fri. 8.15am–7.40pm; Sat. 8.15am–5.40pm
Express delivery 🕐 Mon.–Fri. 8.15am–5.30pm; Sat. 8.15am–noon
Fax, telegrams 🕐 24-hour service
Money orders *piazza Cordusio 3* ☎ 028056812 🕐 Mon.–Fri. 8.30am–5.30pm; Sat. 8.30am–1pm; Sun. 9.45am–3pm

Tourism

[7] Municipal offices *Galleria Vittorio Emanuele II* ☎ 0262083101 🕐 Mon.–Sat. 8.30am–7pm
[8] APT Tourist board

via Marconi 1 ☎ 02725241
[9] Iat Tourist information *via Marconi 1* ☎ 0272524300 🕐 Mon.–Fri. 8.30am–7pm (8pm in summer); Sat. 9am–1pm, 2–6pm (7pm in summer); Sun. 9am–1pm, 2–5pm
[10] TCI Italian Touring Club *corso Italia 10* ☎ 02852 6304 🕐 Mon.–Fri. 9am–7pm; Sat. 9am–1pm, 3–6.30pm

Emergencies

Doctor ☎ 0234567
Ambulance ☎ 118
Pharmacist *Stazione Centrale* ☎ 026690735

Where to stay

Where to stay in Milan

Near the Duomo ➟ 18, 20 or
La Scala ➟ 28, in the city center; in
Sant' Ambrogio ➟ 24 or Cairoli ➟ 28,
in Milan's quaint old quarter; in Piazza
Repubblica ➟ 30, the financial district,
five minutes' from Stazione Centrale;
near the Fiera ➟ 34, 36, 38.

Information on the hotels

The symbols accompanying each hotel tell you, among other things: the number of rooms, the price range for a double room including breakfast and sales tax at 20%, the services and facilities provided by the hotel. A single person occupying a double room can expect to pay about two thirds of the price, though this may rise in high season.

Hotels

THE INSIDER'S FAVORITES

High season

Milan attracts large numbers of visitors during festivals, the April trade fair (the Fiera di Milano) and the February and October fashion shows. During these periods it is difficult to find accommodation unless you have reserved in advance.

Reservations

Reservation service for hotels in the 2- to 5- star categories (toll-free number only operational within Italy):
Centro Prenotazioni Hotel Italia
☎ 167015772   🕐 9am–7pm
APT, the tourist board, provides an exhaustive list of hotels in Milan:
APT via Marconi 1 ☎ 02725241

➤ Where to stay

De La Ville (1)
via Hoepli 6 ☎ 02867651 ➡ 02866609

🅼 *1 Duomo, San Babila; 3 Duomo* 🅿 *109 rooms* ●●●● ▬ 🕐 ▦ *satellite* 🎛 📶 Ⅲ 🍴 *Canova* 🆈 *Visconteo* ♿ 🚿 @ *de.la.ville@italyhotel.com*

A member of the Sina Hotels chain, the De La Ville is ideally situated between the Duomo ➡ 86, la Scala ➡ 88, and via Monte Napoleone ➡ 128, which is one of Milan's most exclusive shopping streets. All the rooms are very tastefully decorated in the style of a 19th-century English manor house, and the suites are richly upholstered in delicate colors, with matching bedspreads and curtains. There are exquisite marble bathrooms. The bar, the Visconteo, makes a perfect meeting place for friends or business associates. Don't miss the hotel's Mediterranean restaurant, the Canova, which offers a first class cuisine and an extensive wine list.

Starhotel Rosa (2)
via Pattari 5 ☎ 028831 ➡ 028057964

🅼 *1 Duomo, San Babila; 3 Duomo* 🅿 *185 rooms* ●●●● ▬ 🕐 ▦ *satellite* 🎛 📶 Ⅲ 🍴 *Il caminetto* 🆈 ❌ ✚

The Starhotel Rosa is very close to elegant corso Vittorio Emanuele II ➡ 122. It has beautiful carpets, wallpaper in pastel shades, and spacious bathrooms which characterize all the rooms and suites. The hotel provides a wide range of additional services to make guests even more comfortable, these include booking theater tickets, arranging guided tours of the city, and babysitting is provided for parents who would like to enjoy an evening out. The ground floor offers a welcoming American bar and a restaurant, the Gourmet, which serves good classic meals. An extensive buffet is provided at breakfast. Eight meeting rooms are available for business guests each holding 20 to 100 people and offering all the latest office facilities.

Jolly President (3)
largo Augusto 10 ☎ (02) 77461 ➡ (02) 783 449

🅼 *1 Duomo, San Babila; 3 Duomo* 🅿 *220 rooms* ●●●● ▬ ▦ *satellite* 🎛 📶 Ⅲ 🍴 *Il Verziere* 🚿 ✚ @ *www.leisureplanet.com; Jollyhac@primopiano.it*

Situated close to piazza San Babila ➡ 124, the Jolly President is primarily a business hotel. It attracts a large number of guests from abroad and offers a wide range of well-equipped function rooms that are suitable for meetings, seminars and large conferences. There is a free shuttle service which runs to Linate Airport on weekdays.

Not forgetting
■ **Grand Hotel Duomo (4)** via San Raffaele 1 ☎ 028833 ➡ 0286462027 ●●●●●
■ **Casa Svizzera (5)** via San Raffaele 3 ☎ 028692246 ➡ 02720 04690 ●●
■ **Galileo (6)** corso Europa 9 ☎ 027743 ➡ 0276020584 ●●●

In the area

The area around via Mazzini and piazza Cordusio is centrally located close to the city's museums and monuments, but also to Brera, near the stock exchange. Full of bars and nightclubs, it will prove irresistible to night-owls. ■ Where to eat ➡ 44 ➡ 64 ■ After dark ➡ 76 ➡ 80

Where to stay

Spadari al Duomo (7)
via Spadari 11 ☎ 0272002371 ➡ 02861184

M / Duomo; 3 Duomo P *39 rooms* ●●● ▣ ◷ *closed at Christmas* ▣ *satellite* ▣ ▐ ▥ ⱬ *grill bar* ▮ ▧ *no large pets*

Tucked away in the historic quarter of the city close to the Duomo ➡ 86, and piazza Cordusio, this unusual hotel is housed in an early 20th-century *palazzo*. The scene is set as soon as you walk through the entrance, with a unique fireplace designed by Giò Pomodoro. Everything here – from the building itself to the furniture and the modern art that adorns the walls – has been carefully thought out and very tastefully executed by local artists and architects. No detail has been left to chance. The light, airy bedrooms are decorated in soft colors and furnished in postmodern style with pale wood. Some rooms are equipped with a jacuzzi. You can choose to take breakfast in your room, or enjoy it in the American bar that has been stylishly decorated by Valentino Viga. This is an hotel that is thoroughly recommended for art-lovers.

Sir Edward (8)
via Mazzini 4 ☎ 02877877 ➡ 02877844

M / Duomo, Cordusio; 3 Duomo P *39 rooms* ●●● ▣ ▣ *satellite* ▣ ▥ ▐ ▥ ▮ ▧ ♿ ✚ @ *sir/edw@bbs.infosquare.it*

In an old *palazzo* that was renovated in 1993, the Sir Edward hotel offers every comfort for guests. The bedrooms, sober and functional yet stylish, are very well equipped and each bathroom has a bath with jacuzzi. The suites even have saunas. The excellent amenities attract many business guests.

Gritti (9)
piazza Santa Maria Beltrade 4 ☎ 02801056 ➡ 0289010999

M / Duomo; 3 Duomo P *48 rooms* ● ▣ ▣ *satellite* ▣ ▐ ▥ ▮ ✚ @ *hotel.gritti@iol.it*

Despite being situated on the busy via Torino, one of the main commercial arteries of Milan, the Gritti hotel, which was fully renovated in 1988, offers an ideal refuge for those wishing to escape the noise and tumult of the city yet who want to stay within its center. The welcoming hotel lobby is huge and is filled with light, the bedrooms are comfortable, and the atmosphere in the bar is informal and relaxed. Although it is centrally located this hotel is still very reasonably priced. A large function room is available for seminars and business meetings.

Not forgetting

■ **Dei Cavalieri (10)** piazza Missori 1 ☎ 0288571 ➡ 0272021683 ●●●
■ **Hotel Brunelleschi (11)** via Baracchini 12 ☎ 028843
➡ 02804924 ●●●

Some of the designer furniture at the Spadari al Duomo: the fireplace by Gio Pomodoro (above) and furniture by Ugo La Pietra (top left).

The area around corso di Porta Romana is crammed with boutiques, bars and theaters. Also in the area is the Università degli Studi. Metro line three provides easy access to the center. ■ Where to eat ➡ 64 ■ After dark ➡ 76 ■ What to see ➡ 92 ■ Where to shop ➡ 124

Where to stay

Hotel Ambrosiano (12)
via Santa Sofia 9 ☎ 0258306044 ➡ 0258305067

M 3 Missori, Crocetta P 78 rooms ●● ▣ ▣ satellite ☎ ▐▌ ▥ ▼ ▨ ✚ ✂ ✦ @ htambros@tin.it

One of the Ambrosiano's major attractions is its central location behind the Milan university, only a few minutes' walk from piazza San Babila, which is a lively area convenient for both interesting cultural sites as well as for shopping. The hotel rooms are very comfortable and quiet with pastel furnishings and elegant bathrooms with marble fittings.
★ Choose a room at the back and you'll have views over the hotel's charming garden. The hotel also has a fitness center that is equipped with weights and other body-building machines.

Lloyd (13)
corso di Porta Romana 48 ☎ 0258303332 ➡ 0258303365

M 3 Crocetta P 57 rooms ●●● ▣ ▣ satellite ☎ ▐▌ ▥ ✚ @ lloydhtl@tin.it

The Lloyd nestles between the boutiques and theaters of corso di Porta Romana, a short distance from piazza del Duomo and the university, opposite the beautiful church of San Nazaro Maggiore ➡ 92. Recently renovated and modernized. The lobby's comfortable armchairs and blue couches match the comfort of the bedrooms. Large public rooms are available for receptions, conferences, meetings, presentations and fashion shows.

Ascot (14)
via Lentasio 3 ☎ 0258303300 ➡ 0258303203

M 3 Missori P 63 rooms ●● ▣ ◷ closed Christmas, Aug. ▣ satellite ☎ ▐▌ ▥ ▼

The Ascot is ideally located, very near the university, and a few hundred yards from piazza Missori and the subway station. Guests can relax in the bar or in the softly-lit lounge with its many armchairs and couches. The rooms are comfortable and modern. There is also a private garage. A pleasant, tranquil stay is guaranteed.

Liberty (15)
viale Bligny 56 ☎ 0258318562 ➡ 0258319061

M 3 Porta Romana P 52 rooms ●● ▣ ▣ satellite ☎ ▐▌ ▥ ▼

This building was once an old apartment block that has been converted into an hotel. It has been furnished throughout – from the reception desk to every guest room, as its name suggests, in Liberty style. It has beautiful marble bathrooms, some with jacuzzi.

Not forgetting
■ **Hotel Canada (16)** via Santa Sofia 16 ☎ 0258304844 ➡ 0258300282 ●●
■ **D'Este (17)** viale Bligny 23 ☎ 0258321001 ➡ 0258321136 ●●●

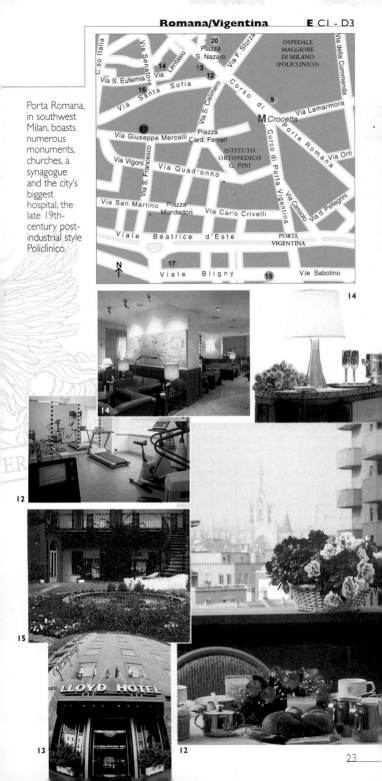

Porta Romana, in southwest Milan, boasts numerous monuments, churches, a synagogue and the city's biggest hospital, the late 19th-century post-industrial style Policlinico.

In the area

Not far from the church of Sant'Ambrogio is historic Milan, its winding streets, studios, boutiques, trattorias and old apartment blocks much favored by young people and artists. ■ Where to eat ➡ 62 ➡ 66 ➡ 70 ■ What to see ➡ 94 ➡ 96 ■ Where to shop ➡ 142 ➡ 144

Where to stay

Pierre (18)
via De Amicis 32 ☎ 0272000581 ➡ 028052157

🔲 94 🅿 *49 rooms* ●●●● 🔲 🔲 *closed Christmas, New Year, Aug.* 🔲 *satellite* 🔲 🔢 🔢 🔢 🔢 *Petit Pierre* 🔲 🔲 🔲 🔲 @ *www. hotelpierre.it; photel@punto.it*

The Pierre, at the top of a charming street, occupies two small 18th-century mansions. The hotel has been lovingly and tastefully restored, and has preserved its period furniture and old-style charm. However, it still provides all the modern comforts that you would expect to find in any top hotel. The soft lighting in the reception area is warm and welcoming and shows to advantage the beautiful marble decor and the coffered ceiling. The bedrooms are soothing and peaceful and have marble bathrooms with elegant, monogramed bathroom accessories. ★ A big breakfast buffet is served under the splendid Liberty-style glass roof of the Petit Pierre restaurant. A delightful and comfortable hotel.

Ariston (19)
largo Carrobbio 2 ☎ 02720 00556 ➡ 0272000914

🅼 *3 Duomo* 🅿 *46 rooms* ●● 🔲 🔲 *closed Aug.* 🔲 *satellite* 🔲 🔢 🔢 🔲 @ *www.cityhightsnews.com/ariston.htm*

This hotel is a must for all nature lovers and environmentalists. Everything at the Ariston is green, from the interiors and the walls to the wooden furniture. The rooms are all equipped with ion-emitting machines which purify the air, the lamps have energy-saving bulbs, and every scrap of paper is recycled. Drinks and herbal teas are made with filtered water and at breakfast guests can help themselves to various bio products as well as the usual traditional breakfast foods. A whole floor is set aside for non-smokers. In addition, just to show that their concern for ecology does not stop at the hotel door, the owners even hire out bikes to residents who wish to take some exercise and also explore the area without polluting the atmosphere.

Regina (20)
via Cesare Correnti 13 ☎ 0258106913 ➡ 0258107033

🔲 *2, 14* 🅿 *43 rooms* ●● 🔲 🔲 *closed Christmas–Jan. 6, Aug.* 🔲 *satellite* 🔲 🔢 🔢 🔢 🔲 @ *hotel.regina@traveleurope.it*

The Regina is in via Cesare Correnti, which is one of Milan's busy shopping streets, not far from the Colonne di San Lorenzo ➡ 94, the lively area of Porta Ticinese ➡ 142 and the colorful Navigli district with its canals and nightlife. The enormous lobby with its pastel decor is lit by a beautiful chandelier and evokes a retro-style atmosphere. The rooms are cozy and attractively furnished, and the sheets are pure linen.

Not forgetting

■ **Mentana** (21) via Morigi 2 piazza Mentana ☎ 0286454255 ➡ 02865 382 ●

The light and airy veranda of the Petit Pierre restaurant is an oasis of calm away from the bustle of the city.

25

rea

a number of hotels near Castello Sforzesco ➡ 98 and Parco
99, just off the pedestrianized via Dante, one of Milan's
shopping streets. ■ Where to eat ➡ 48 ■ After dark ➡ 74
■ What to see ➡ 96 ➡ 98 ➡ 100 ■ Where to shop ➡ 140

➤ Where to stay

Radisson SAS Bonaparte Hotel Milano (22)
via Cusani 13 ☎ 028560 ➡ 028693601

Ⓜ / Cairoli 🅿 **65 rooms** ●●●● ◫ 📺 satellite 🔆 📶 🎚 🍴 Il Filarete ✚

The Bonaparte hotel is part of the Radisson SAS hotel chain. It is
housed in a modern building opposite Castello Sforzesco ➡ 98, a
few minutes' walk from the Brera district ➡ 100, a popular haunt of
artists and is full of late night bars and fashionable restaurants. The
hotel rooms and suites are modern, spacious and soundproof. Service
is courteous and personal. The hotel's amenities, meeting rooms and
range of facilities make it an ideal choice for business guests. There
are private parking facilities.

London (23)
via Rovello 3 ☎ 0272020166 ➡ 028057037

Ⓜ / Cairoli 🅿 **29 rooms** ● ◫ 📺 satellite 🔆 🎚 🍷 🈲 🚫
@ hotel.london@traveleurope.it

This small friendly hotel, only a few minutes' walk from la Scala ➡ 74
➡ 88, Castello Sforzesco ➡ 98 and the Piccolo Teatro ➡ 76, is a haven
of peace, away from the noise and bustle of the city traffic. The small,
charming hotel lobby with its charming bar, lovely old fireplace and
comfortable velvet armchairs sets the tone. The large bedrooms have
light wood furnishings and a quiet cozy atmosphere. Breakfast is brought
to your room.

Cairoli (24)
via Porlezza 4 ☎ 02801371 ➡ 0272002243

Ⓜ / Cairoli 🅿 **38 rooms** ● ◫ 📺 satellite 🔆 📶 🎚

The Cairoli is tucked away down a little pedestrianized stone-paved
street, close to via Dante. Nearby is Castello Sforzesco ➡ 98, and a
few streets away is the Borsa (stock exchange) in piazza degli Affari.
Each of the rooms is individually decorated with floral wallpaper and
marble fittings. A peaceful stay is guaranteed – a rare privilege in Milan's
historic center.

Star (25)
via dei Bossi 5 ☎ 02801501 ➡ 02861787

Ⓜ / Cordusio **30 rooms** ●● 🕒 closed August, Christmas ◫ 🔆 📶 📺 🎚
@ www.starhotel.it ; Information@starhotel.it

The Star is situated in a charming and quiet street, close to La Scala.
Friendly reception, excellent service and top-quality facilities. For those
looking for the ultimate in relaxation, some rooms are equipped with a
multi-function shower and a sauna.

Not forgetting
■ **King (26)** corso Magenta 19 ☎ 02874432 ➡ 0289010798 ●●

Piazza Castello — 38 37
Piazza Castello
22
Via dell'Orso
14
M Cadorna
Via dell'Orso
Piazzale Cadorna
Via Ricasoli
M Cairoli
Via Cusani
Via Lauro
Largo Cairoli
Via Rovello
Via Broletto
Via d. Bossi
26
Via Carducci
62
Via S. Nicolao
TEATRO DAL VERME
Via Illica
Via Puccini
23
Via Dante
Via S. Giovanni sul Muro
24
Via Porlezza
Via Camperio
4
35
Corso
59
Magenta
Via Meravigli
Piazza Cordusio
Cordusio **M**
36 3 58 25 60
BORSA
N

22

22

24

23

What better place to stay than near La Scala ➡ 74, ➡ 88, one of the world's great opera houses. Close by there are exclusive streets housing top fashion boutiques, and piazza Cavour where a number of newspapers have their head offices. ■ Where to eat ➡ 46

➡ Where to stay

27
27
27

Four Seasons (27)
via Gesù 8 ☎ 0277088 ➡ 0277085000

M 3 Montenapoleone **P** *98 rooms* ●●●●● ☐ 🖵 *satellite* 🕿 📶 Ⅲ
📶 *Il Teatro, La Veranda* **Y** *Il Foyer* 🚿 🍽 ✚ 🍴 🌟 🌿 🎵
@ www.fourseasons.com

This former convent, built in the 15th-century and lavishly restored, now houses one of the city's most prestigious hotels. This is where movie stars, big company bosses and executives stay. The rooms are extremely comfortable, spacious and elegant with sycamore-wood furniture and Fortuny drapes. ★ The 28 suites, which occupy the former cells, overlook the old cloister where guests can admire fragments of medieval frescos. The hotel has two restaurants: La Veranda, ideal for a light snack, and Il Teatro (open only in the evenings), which has a more intimate atmosphere and serves classic Italian cuisine and wine. The bar, Il Foyer, has a large fireplace and is decorated with sets from La Scala ➡ 74, ➡ 88, designed by Peroni.

Grand Hotel et de Milan (28)
via Manzoni 29 ☎ 02723141 ➡ 0286460861

M *I Duomo* ; *3 Montenapoleone* **P** *95 rooms* ●●●●● ☐ ① 🖵 *satellite*
🕿 📶 Ⅲ 📶 *Caruso, Don Carlos* **Y** 🚿 @ www.madeinitaly.com/sdm/milan;
hotel.milan@galaktica.it

The Grand Hotel's prime location next to La Scala ➡ 74, ➡ 88 has earned it the patronage of many celebrities, divas, royals and well-known figures, among them Richard Wagner, Pietro Mascagni, Ernest Hemingway,

■ What to see ➡
88, ➡ 90 ■ Where
to shop ➡ 128,
➡ 132

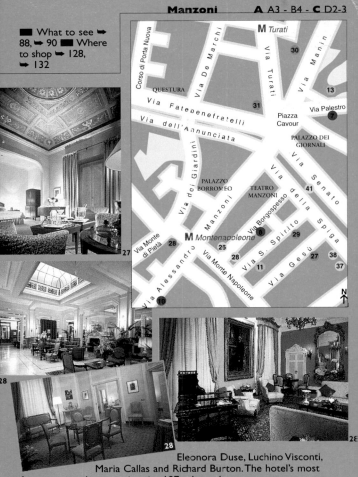

Eleonora Duse, Luchino Visconti,
Maria Callas and Richard Burton. The hotel's most
famous room, however, is suite 107, where the great composer,
Giuseppe Verdi, lived for some time up until his death. The hotel oozes
19th-century luxury: the lobby with its paneling, brasses and marble
mosaic flooring, the elegant Camino room, lit by a splendid Liberty-style
chandelier and the rooms with their old-style furnishings and marble
bathrooms. The Don Carlos restaurant, intimate yet theatrical, is ideal
for a private tête-à-tête, while the Caruso, open at midday, is the perfect
venue for a working lunch.

Manzoni (29)
via Santo Spirito 20 ☎ 0276005700 ➡ 02784212

Ⓜ 3 Montenapoleone Ⓟ *52 rooms* ●● ▤ ▣ *satellite* ▨ Ⓨ

Tucked away off the busy via Monte Napoleone and via Manzoni, this
hotel, with its lovely, soundproofed rooms, promises a quiet, comfortable
stay in historic Milan. The bathrooms are enormous, airy and light. The
big breakfasts are served in the bar.

Not forgetting
■ **Manin (30)** via Manin 7 ☎ 02659 6511 ➡ 02655 2160 ●●●
■ **Cavour (31)** via Fatebenefratelli 21 ☎ 02657 2051 ➡ 02659 2263 ●●

In the area

Spread out around piazza della Repubblica is Milan's financial and business district, which sprang up in the 1950s and 1960s. The area is only five minutes' walk from Stazione Centrale. ■ Where to eat ➡ 52 ■ What to see ➡ 90

➤ Where to stay

Principe di Savoia (32)
piazza della Repubblica 17 ☎ 0262301 ➡ 026595838

Ⓜ *3 Repubblica* 🅿 *299 rooms* ●●●●● ▭ ▣ *satellite* ☎ ▮▮ Ⅲ ▥ *Galleria* ▮ ⚿ ✗ ✚ ≋ ✂ ✴ ♪ @ *www.ittsheraton.com*

Occupying a *palazzo* built in 1927 and completely renovated, the Principe di Savoia is truly the prince of hotels. The imposing neoclassical façade conceals an elegant interior: marble bathrooms, enormous rooms furnished with antiques and valuable rugs. ★ The hotel also boasts an indoor pool, a solarium, a fitness center and a beauty salon. Its Liberty-style restaurant, the Galleria, serves first class Italian cuisine and delicious Lombard specialties.

Palace (33)
piazza della Repubblica 20 ☎ 026336 ➡ 02654485

Ⓜ *3 Repubblica* 🅿 *216 rooms* ●●●●● ▭ ▣ *satellite* ☎ ▮▮ Ⅲ ▥ *Casanova Grill* ▮ ⚿ ✗ ✚ @ *www.luxorycollection.com/palacemilano*

The interior behind this majestic pink and gray marble façade does not disappoint; this is a top-notch hotel, recently renovated and belonging to the same chain as its neighbor, the Principe di Savoia. It offers its cosmopolitan clientele all the comforts you would expect of a palace and attracts wealthy business guests from the world of finance who know that they can be assured of a high standard of service and amenities. The rooms are elegant, in muted shades, with stuccoed

ceilings and early 19th-century style furnishings. The hotel boasts a very fine restaurant, the Casanova Grill, which combines traditional and modern cuisine.

Diana Majestic (34)
viale Piave 42 ☎ 02295 13404 ➠ 02201 072

M / Porta Venezia **P** *94 rooms* ●●●● ▣ ◷ *closed Aug.* ▣ *satellite*
☎ ▐ 🍴 *La Veranda* ▼ ✖ ✚ ★ @ *www.sheraton.com/dianamajestic*

The name of this hotel comes from the 'Diana Baths', the first swimming pool in Italy for women, opened in Milan in 1842. Its recent restoration has preserved the art deco architecture. Stamped with the charm of a turn of the century *palazzo*, the hotel is very popular with designers and models during the season of the big fashion shows. On the ground floor, guests can enjoy the charm and quiet of the public rooms, furnished with 1930s style leather armchairs, and also the large round lounge with its cane chairs, overlooking the garden. Despite the addition of modern comforts, time seems to stand still in the bedrooms, furnished with period and antique furniture. This hotel is a must for anyone nostalgic for the *belle époque*.

Not forgetting
■■■ **Jolly Touring (35)** via Tarchetti 2 ☎ 026335 ➠ 02659 2209 ●●●
■■■ **Duca di Milano (36)** piazza della Repubblica 13 ☎ 026284
➠ 02655 5966 ●●●●●

34

33

34

HOTEL DIANA MAJESTIC MILANO

33

A hotel near Stazione Centrale, Milan's main railway station, is worth considering if you're arriving by rail or air (trains for the airport leave from Stazione Centrale). The station's imposing architecture, designed by Ulisse Stacchini, is worth a detour in itself, as is the Pirelli skyscraper

Where to stay

Excelsior Gallia (37)
piazza Duca d'Aosta 9 ☎ 026785 ➡ 0266713239

Ⓜ 2 Centrale F.S.; 3 Centrale F.S. Ⓟ **237 rooms** ●●●● ▭ ▣ satellite 🖻 🛅 ▥
🍴 Gallia's restaurant ▮ ▮ ▮ ✚ ✂ ♫ @ 106340.2331@compuserve.com

This hotel, opened in the 1930s, quickly built up an affluent clientele from those arriving in Milan by train, and has played host to many celebrities. The lobby is luxurious and elegant, and the tasteful 1930s, 1950s and contemporary furnishings in the rooms, the good sized bathrooms and the fine bedlinen are all proof of a concern for quality in all areas and the comfort and well-being of the hotel's guests. Sample the delicious cuisine in the top class restaurant or relax with a cocktail in the Baboon Bar. ★ From the top floor there are good views over the green roofs of the station. The Excelsior Gallia offers relaxed, elegant surroundings and prompt, efficient service. It also has a well-equipped fitness center.

Michelangelo (38)
via Scarlatti 33 ☎ 026755 ➡ 026694232

Ⓜ 1 Lima Ⓟ **300 rooms** ●●●● ▭ Ⓞ closed Aug. ▣ satellite 🖻 🛅 ▥
🍴 Il Ghirlandaio ▮ ✚ conference center with 1,300 places

The Michelangelo hotel was completely renovated in 1992. Behind its pink façade the proprietors run a modern and very professional hotel. The rooms, in soft, pastel shades, are furnished with modern or walnut period furniture and hung with plush drapes. All the bathrooms are bright and cheerful and have jacuzzis. The stylish restaurant, called Il Ghirlandaio, has a cozy atmosphere and serves delicate dishes in the traditional Italian style as well as excellent international cusine. The lounge bar is bright and spacious. The hotel has a wide range of amenities and business services and is well equipped for conferences and seminars.

Hilton (39)
via Galvani 12 ☎ 0269831 ➡ 0266710810

Ⓜ 2 Centrale F.S.; 3 Centrale F.S. Ⓟ **321 rooms** ●●●● ▭ ▣ satellite 🖻 🛅
▥ 🍴 da Giuseppe, Terrazza Valentino ▮ ▮ ✚ ▦ @ www.hilton.com

Guests are guaranteed a warm reception and efficient service in keeping with the reputation of the well known international chain of luxury Hilton hotels. The comfortable rooms are designed to please even the most demanding guests and many have recently been renovated. Residents can breakfast in the cozy surroundings of the restaurant, da Giuseppe, which also serves Milanese specialties at lunchtime and in the evenings. The hotel's other restaurant, Terrazza Valentino, is more suited to business lunches and dinners.

Not forgetting

■ **Madison (40)** via Gasparotto 8 ☎ 02669 87965 ➡ 02670 75059 ●●
■ **Bristol (41)** via Scarlatti 32 ☎ 02669 4141 ➡ 02670 2942 ●●

opposite, designed
by Gio Ponti.
■ Where to eat
➥ 54

Map labels:
Via Melchiorre Gioia
Via P. Seveso
Via Soperga
Macchi
Piazza Caiazzo
M Sondrio
Via Copernico
Via F. Filzi
STAZIONE CENTRALE
Piazza Luigi di Savoia
Caiazzo M
Via Andrea Doria
Via Mauro
Via Settembrini
40
Piazza V Novembre
41
38
39   37
Piazza Duca d'Aosta
Via Galvani
M Centrale   Via Vitruvio

ALBERGO GALLIA

37

37

37

A number of luxury
hotels have grown
up around Milan's
Stazione Centrale.

38

39

40

33

In the area

There is no shortage of hotels in the area around the bustling via Paolo Sarpi, near the Fiera, and around Milan's 'Chinatown', where Chinese restaurants and fur and leather goods stores abound. ■ Where to eat ➡ 60

Where to stay

Hermitage (42)
via Messina 10 ☎ 0233107700, 0233107399

🔲 *12, 14, 29, 30, 33, 94* 🅿 *131 rooms* ●●● ▭ ▣ *satellite* 📷 📠
🍴 *Il Sambuco* ➡ *58* 🍸 *Il Patio (summer only), Caesar's Bar* ✛ ✠

The latest addition to the Monrif chain is a very stylish hotel. The lobby, with its checkered flooring, is large and welcoming; the rooms are simply but very tastefully furnished and are more than comfortable. The hotel has 12 suites and all guests have access to the pleasant conservatory. The hotel's impressive conference center and banqueting room, which can hold up to 200 people, make it an ideal venue for large meetings. Besides being popular with the business community, the hotel also hosts many people from the design and fashion world. Make sure that you visit the hotel's two relaxing and pleasant bars, Il Patio and Caesar's. The excellent restaurant which specializes in fish dishes, Il Sambuco ➡ 58, is one of Milan's finest and is definitely well worth a visit.

Grand Hotel Fieramilano (43)
viale Boezio 20 ☎ 02336221 ➡ 02314119

🔲 *19, 27* 🅿 *238 rooms* ●●● ▭ ▣ 📷 📠 ▥ 🍴 *Ambrosiano* 🍸 ✛ ✠

Situated opposite the Fiera exhibition ground (the Domodossola entrance), the Grand Hotel Fieramilano, a vast modern complex, is the ideal location for business people who want to be as close as possible to the trade fairs. The rooms are comfortable and the service is slick and efficient. Breakfast is served in a pleasant conservatory. Spacious and surprisingly peaceful.

Admiral (44)
via Domodossola 16 ☎ 023492151 ➡ 0233106660

🔲 *19, 27* 🅿 *60 rooms* ●● ▭ 🕐 *closed Aug.* ▣ *satellite* 📷 📠 ▥
🍸 ✛ 🎵 @ *www.admiralhotel.it*

The already spacious hotel rooms, with their 18th-century decor, are further extended by a small anteroom. In summer, you can enjoy the balcony overlooking the Fiera. Bathrooms are all of the highest standard and are comfortable and well equipped. The hotel can organize special functions on request, provide secretarial or translation services and even organize city tours or excursions to places of interest outside Milan. There is a large breakfast buffet. The Admiral hotel is ideal if you are looking for reasonably priced but comfortable accommodation near the Fiera.

Not forgetting

■ **Poliziano (45)** via Poliziano 11 ☎ 0233602494 ➡ 0233106410 ●●
■ **Mozart (46)** piazza Gerusalemme 6 ☎ 0233104215
➡ 0233103231 ●●

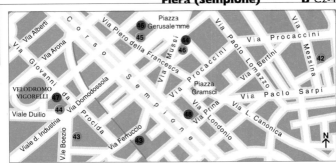

42

43

43

Grand Hotel Fieramilano
★★★★

43

44

44

Basic facts

The area around the Fiera and the Meazza stadium ➡ 106 receives one and a half million visitors each year. These charming hotels with their unbeatable prices are havens of peace away from the noise and crowds. It's easy to get into the center from here by public transport.

Where to stay

Montebianco (47)
via Monte Rosa 90 ☎ **(02) 480 12130** ➡ **(02) 480 00658**

Ⓜ *1 Lotto* Ⓟ *44 rooms* ● ⊟ 💻 *satellite* 🛎 Ⅲ ⅰ ✦ ✦

Housed in an elegant villa in a quiet residential street, the Montebianco hotel is very conveniently located near the ring roads and Autostrada, the exhibition center, the Palalido and the Meazza stadium ➡ 106. The hotel's public areas are large and welcoming, and the bedrooms are well kept and very comfortable. There are rooms available for business meetings and all residents have access to the private garage and a pretty garden which is paricularly pleasant in the summer. There is also a charming breakfast room.

Monterosa (48)
piazzale Lotto 14 ☎ **(02) 392 62170** ➡ **(02) 392 62212**

Ⓜ *1 Lotto* Ⓟ *Secure garage* *27 rooms* ● ⊟ 💻 *satellite* 🛎 ⅰ Ⅲ
ⅰ *Picanha's*

The Monterosa is a few hundred yards from the Fiera, very near the subway station, the Palalido and the Meazza stadium ➡ 106. This quiet and comfortable small hotel has recently been renovated. Its Brazilian restaurant, which is often frequented by non-residents, will add an exotic flavor to your stay.

Domenichino (49)
via Domenichino 41 ☎ **(02) 480 09692** ➡ **(02) 480 03953**

Ⓜ *1 Amendola-Fiera* Ⓟ *78 rooms* ● ⊟ 🕐 *closed New Year's Eve, Aug.*
💻 *satellite* 🛎 ⅰ Ⅲ ⅰ ✦

A modern hotel located in a residential street, the Domenichino does everything possible to make its guests feel completely comfortable and relaxed. The atmosphere is warm and welcoming and the rooms are simply and attractively furnished. There is an excellent sweet and savory breakfast buffet.

Mini Hotel Portello (50)
via Guglielmo Silva 12 ☎ **(02) 481 4944** ➡ **(02) 481 9243**

📷 *78* Ⓟ *96 rooms* ● ⊟ 🕐 *closed Christmas–Epiphany, Aug.* 💻 *satellite* 🛎
Ⅲ ⅰ ✦

Near the new Portello pavilion, the latest addition to the Fiera, the Mini Hotel Portello hosts many business travelers. Its facilities include a meeting room and a private garage. The bedrooms are modern and very well equipped.

Not forgetting

■ **Fiera (51)** via Spinola 9 ☎ (02) 480 05472 ➡ (02) 480 08494 ●

Moderately priced hotels with good facilities are plentiful between Lotto and Amendola, near the Fiera.

In the area

On the fringes of the Fiera and Magenta districts is the city's most upmarket residential area. Business people and tourists staying here are near the exhibition centers and the splendid houses and elegant shopping streets of wealthy Milan. ■ Where to eat ➡ 70

Where to stay

Ramada Grand Hotel (52)
via Giorgio Washington 66 ☎ 0248521 ➡ 024818925

🔲 61 🅿 323 rooms ●●● ▭ ▣ satellite ☎ 🔲 Ⅲ 🔲 La Brasserie de Milan 🔲 🔲 🔲

An immense modern building, resembling an American skyscraper, houses the Ramada Grand Hotel. It has a beautiful spacious lobby and first class rooms. The restaurant, the Brasserie de Milan, with its attractive blue and yellow decor, serves traditional Lombard specialties that are actually prepared in full view of the diners. Equipped with the most up-to-date facilities, the hotel is an ideal venue for meetings, conferences and seminars and is able to meet all the needs and requirements of the business traveler.

Capitol (53)
via Cimarosa 6 ☎ 0248003050 ➡ 024694724

🔲 I Pagano 🅿 95 rooms ●● ▭ 🔲 closed Aug. ▣ satellite ☎ 🔲 Ⅲ
🔲 L'Angolo 🔲 🔲@ www.milanlorencehotel.it; capitol@tol.it

If you are staying at the Capitol hotel, which is located at the heart of the Magenta district, make sure you visit the Church of Santa Maria delle Grazie ➡ 96 and do some window shopping on corso Vercelli. The hotel staff are very helpful and all the rooms are extremely comfortable and well equipped. Ask for a room at the back of the hotel as these are much quieter. The Angolo restaurant serves good local specialties.

Washington (54)
via Giorgio Washington 23 ☎ 024813216 ➡ 024814761

🔲 61 🅿 34 rooms ●●● ▭ ▣ satellite ☎ 🔲 Ⅲ 🔲
@ www.hotelwashington@traveleurope.it

The Washington occupies a 19th-century neo-Renaissance apartment block in a quiet, pretty residential street, not far from the Fiera district. There is a shuttle service to the exhibition centers and into the city center. The good-sized rooms are simple and comfortable, and some have a terrace. A traditional *prima colazione* is served in the spacious breakfast room.

Metrò (55)
corso Vercelli 61 ☎ 02468704 ➡ 0248010295

🔲 I Conciliazione 🅿 37 rooms ● ▭ 🔲 ☎ 🔲 Ⅲ

Recently restored, the hotel Metrò's rooms are attractive, spacious, well-furnished and have modern bathrooms. ★ The charming rooms on the top floor, complete with their sloping roofs and jacuzzis, are especially popular and cozy.

Not forgetting

■ **Mini Tiziano (56)** via Tiziano 6 ☎ 024699035 ➡ 024812153 ●

■ What to see ➥ 76

Map labels:
Piazza Buonarroti — 55 — Largo Zandonai
M *Buonarroti*
Via San Siro
Via M. Buonarroti
Via Pier Capponi
Via Giotto
Pagano **M**
M *Wagner*
75 Via Marghera
55
Corso Vercelli
7 Piazza Piemonte
Via Seprio
Via Sardegna
Via Elba
Via Cimarosa
53
Via Paolo Giovio
Piazza Sicilia
Via Giorgio Washington
Via Salutati
Via Trieste
54
Via Verga
Via S. Caboto
Piazza Po
Via S. Eusebio
Piazza Irnerio
Via Boni
Via Digione
52
Via Egadi
Piazza Vesuvio
N ↑

52

52

52

53

Hotel Capitol

53

HOTEL METRÓ

55

54

Via Giorgio Washington runs from the Fiera in the north to Navigli in the south.

In the area

Although the Certosa district is a little way out of the center, it has a number of pleasant hotels. Just behind the Fiera exhibition ground and close to the major road links with Turin and Venice, this could be an ideal place to break your journey.

▶ Where to stay

Regency (57)
via Arimondi 12 ☎ 0239216021 ➡ 0239217734

🔲 *1, 12, 69* 🅿 *59 rooms* ●●● ▢ 🕔 *closed Aug.* 🖵 *satellite* 🖺 🔧 Ⅲ ⅄
🏃 🚳 *no large pets* ✚ @ *regencyhotel@virtualia.it*

Built in the last century when this area northwest of Milan was still open countryside, the Regency hotel occupies an elegant, stately residence which has an air of intimacy and grandeur that has been conserved by recent renovation work. Peaceful and opulent, this charming hotel has an attractive lobby with a fireplace, very welcoming bedrooms, and luxurious marble bathrooms. It has a selection of function rooms which can be used for meetings, seminars and conferences.

Antares Accademia (58)
viale Certosa 68 ☎ 0239211122 ➡ 0233103878

🔲 *14* 🅿 *67 rooms* ●●● ▢ 🖵 *satellite* 🖺 🔧 Ⅲ 🍴 *Nama* ⅄ 🏃 ✚
@ *antares.hotel.accademia@traveleurope.it*

An imposing statue of Ferruccio Prini graces the lobby of the Antares Accademia. This is an hotel where art is given pride of place. The comfortable rooms are individually decorated with blue and green frescos and *trompe l'oeils* by Angelo La Pica. Some rooms are reserved for non-smokers. The Atares also caters for business guests and has a number of well-equipped function rooms.

Raffaello (59)
viale Certosa 108 ☎ 02327 0146 ➡ 02327 0440

🔲 *14* 🅿 *142 rooms* ●● ▢ 🕔 *closed Christmas–Jan. 6, Aug.* 🖵 *satellite*
🖺 🔧 Ⅲ ✚ @ *hotel_raffaello@iol.it*

The Raffaello is a peaceful hotel set in attractive gardens away from the bustle of the city. Behind its white façade guests will be greeted with a friendly welcome and professional, courteous service. A number of conference rooms and meeting rooms are available for business guests.

Accursio (60)
viale Certosa 88 ☎ 0233001270 ➡ 0239217466

🔲 *14* 🅿 *27 rooms* ● ▢ 🖵 *satellite* 🖺 🔧 Ⅲ

Easy to get to and only a short distance from the Fiera, the Accursio hotel is very convenient for visitors who are passing through Milan. Although small, the rooms are comfortable, well-kept, and attractively furnished, with pleasant bathrooms.

Not forgetting

■ **Mirage (61)** via Casella 61 viale Certosa ☎ 0239210471
➡ 0239210589 ●●

All major routes going west converge on viale Certosa, which runs into the city center.

Where to eat

Late-night eating

However late you come out of the theater or movie theater, you can usually find a pizzeria that is still open and serving food. Some stay open as late as 2am.

Italian coffee

In Italy there are many ways to drink coffee – *caffè* (espresso), *caffè ristretto* (strong espresso), *caffè corretto* (coffee with a liqueur such as grappa, sambuca or brandy), *caffè americano* (weak black coffee), *caffè freddo* (cold coffee), *macchiato* (espresso with a drop of milk), *caffè latte* (milky coffee), *cappuccino*….

Opening hours

Lunch is typically served from midday to 3pm and dinner from 7.30 to 11pm. Since restaurants in Milan tend to have the same opening times, we show alongside each restaurant in this guide only the days and periods of the year during which they are closed.

Gastronomic tradition

Milanese cuisine is among the finest and most innovative in Italy. The traditional *osteria* (inn) and *trattoria* (small restaurant) may be disappearing, but top chefs are stepping in and serving up their own version of Milanese classics such as *risotto giallo* (rice with saffron) and *ossobuco* (goat's shank).

75
Restaurants

THE INSIDER'S FAVORITES

Where to eat

Boeucc (1)
piazza Belgioioso 2 ☎ 02020224

Ⓜ *1 Duomo; 3 Duomo, Montenapoleone* **Lombard and traditional Italian cuisine** ●●●● ▢ 🕐 *Mon.–Fri., Sun. lunch; closed Christmas, New Year, Easter, Aug.*

The first floor (formerly the stables) of the majestic 18th-century *palazzo* Belgioioso houses the historic Boeucc restaurant. People from the world of finance and members of the fashion set come here to enjoy a truly classic Lombard cuisine. There is a wide choice of meat and fish dishes and an excellent wine list. In summer diners can eat outside on the veranda.

Bistrot Duomo (2)
via San Raffaele 2 ☎ 02877120

Ⓜ *1 Duomo; 3 Duomo* **Lombard cuisine** ●●● ▢ 🕐 *Mon. eve.–Sat.; closed Aug.*

Occupying the eighth floor of the building that houses the department store Rinascente ➡ 120, the Bistrot di Gualtiero Marchesi has the most beautiful view over the city and the 130-odd spires of the Duomo. One of Italy's most famous chefs, Gualtiero Marchesi, left his mark in this restaurant before moving to the shores of Lake Iseo. His legacy is a cuisine that combines creativity (ravioli filled with fish, served with a sea bass sauce, fish carpaccio) with respect for Lombard tradition (*ossobuco, cotoletta alla milanese*). The wine list is more modest. Don't miss the delicious desserts.

Savini (3)
Galleria Vittorio Emanuele II ☎ 0272003433

Ⓜ *1 Duomo* **Lombard and international cuisine** ●●●●● ▢
🕐 *Mon.–Fri., Sat. eve.; closed Aug. 3–23*

Beneath the huge metal and glass roof of the Galleria Vittorio Emanuele II ➡ 86, the Savini restaurant (established in 1867) is a temple of cuisine. Its sumptuous interior, with paneling, velvet and period furnishings, is well worth the visit in itself. In summer you can eat outside in the Galleria; the tables are separated off from passers-by with elegant potted plants. The cuisine is international, but is enriched with subtle Lombard flavors. There is an excellent wine list.

Not forgetting

■ **Biffi Scala (4)** via Filodrammatici 2 ☎ 02866651 ●●●● *Classic Italian and international cuisine; one of the best restaurants in the Lombard capital. Much frequented by opera-goers.*
■ **Peck (5)** via Victor Hugo 4 ☎ 02876774 ●●●● *Lombard cuisine. A Milanese institution. Combines tradition, creativity and innovation. The wine list boasts over 300 wines. You can also buy prepared foods to take out.*
■ **Al Mercante (6)** piazza Mercanti 17 ☎ 028052198 ●● *Traditional Italian cuisine. Especially enjoyable in summer when you can eat outside in the piazza surrounded by old Renaissance palazzi.*

Via Andegari

Via Alessandro Manzoni

Via Morone

PALAZZO BELGIOIOSO

9

21
23

1 Piazza Meda

Via Case Rotte

Via Verdi

Via Hoepli

7
8
1
4

2

Piazza della Scala

10

Via Agnello

Via Marino

85

Via S. Dalmazio

Via Silvio Pellico

4

3

Via S. Raffaele

Via Foscolo

5

2

1

4

3

Via T. Grossi

17

M Duomo

Piazza del Duomo

75

M Cordusio

Piazza Cordusio

8

5

Via Orefici

M Duomo

74

5

Via Cantù

Via Spadari

7

8

Via Mazzini

Via Torino

Via Moneta

6

9

22

1

Tradition and quality at Savini in the Galleria Vittorio Emanuele 1.

2

3

3

3

In the area

Some of the most beautiful buildings in Milan are found along via Manzoni from piazza della Scala to piazza Cavour. Opposite via Montenapoleone is Aldo Rossi's fountain, dedicated to the former president of the Republic, Sandro Pertini. ■ Where to stay ➡ 28 ■ What to see ➡ 88 ➡ 90

Where to eat

Terrazza (7)
via Palestro 2 ☎ 0276002186

Ⓜ I Palestro **Mediterranean cuisine** ●●● ⬜ ◌ *Mon. eve.–Sat.; closed Christmas, New Year, Jan. 6, Aug. 8–24*

Housed in the Swiss consulate building, the Terrazza restaurant serves excellent Mediterranean fish dishes in a light and airy modern setting. ★ The restaurant has lovely views over the park and in summer diners can escape the heat of the city and sit outside on the terrace (from which the restaurant gets its name) in the shade of fragrant chestnut trees. Attentive and efficient service.

Bice (8)
via Borgospesso 12 ☎ 0276002572

Ⓜ 3 Montenapoleone **Tuscan cuisine** ●●●● ⬜ ◌ *Tue.–Sun.; closed Christmas–Jan. 6, Easter, Aug.*

Of all the regional cuisines that are available in Milan, Tuscan cuisine is the best represented. Bice is one of the most innovative of the restaurants set up by a group of Tuscan restaurateurs who brought their culinary traditions to the Lombard capital in the 1920s. Now in the hands of the next generation, the Bice restaurant continues to serve up food prepared in the traditional Tuscan way. The wine list includes the best Tuscan wines: chianti, montepulciano, brunello di Montalcino. Diners are made to feel really at home and the service is friendly and faultless.

Bagutta (9)
via Bagutta 14 ☎ 0276002767

Ⓜ I San Babila **Tuscan and traditional cuisine** ●●●● ⬜ ◌ *Mon.–Sat.; closed Christmas–Jan. 6, Aug.*

Situated in a quiet street that is full of antique dealers, the Bagutta restaurant has been serving Tuscan cuisine since the 1920s. It became famous in 1927 when a number of regular customers – writers, artists and publishers – decided to create a literary prize and called it the 'Bagutta'. The restaurant has gone more upmarket since then and businessmen have replaced the men of letters. However, some of the memories are still there: copies of all the books that have won the prize are kept in the front restaurant and on the walls of the main restaurant hangs a large collection of paintings, including 170 caricatures by Mario Vellani Marchi, one of the restaurant's regulars. There is a good choice of wines, especially Tuscan ones.

Not forgetting

■ **Don Lisander (10)** via Manzoni 12 ☎ 0276020130 ●●● *Traditional Italian cuisine and elegant service. Magnificent garden, in the heart of the historic center.* ■ **Saint Andrew's (11)** via Sant'Andrea 23 ☎ 0276023132 ●●●●● *Refined atmosphere of an English gentlemen's club; traditional Italian cuisine.*

■ Where to shop
➡ 124 ➡ 128 ➡ 130
➡ 132

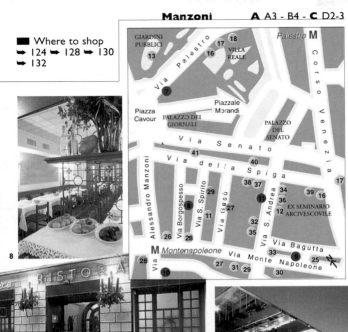

GIARDINI PUBBLICI
13
Via Palestro
17 16
18
VILLA REALE
Palestro **M**
7
Corso Venezia
Piazza Cavour
PALAZZO DEI GIORNALI
Piazzale Morandi
PALAZZO DEL SENATO
Via Senato
41
Via della Spiga
40
Alessandro Manzoni
Via Borgospesso
6
Via S. Spirito
29
11
Via Gesù
27
38 37
Via S. Andrea
13
34
36
12
EX SEMINARIO ARCIVESCOVILE
39
16
17
26
28
32
35
Via Bagutta
M Montenapoleone   Via Monte Napoleone
33
9
25
28
Via
10
27 31 29
30

8

7

9

Bagutta, once a small trattoria, is now famous thanks to the Bagutta literary prize.

9

Brera was once the 'artists' quarter'. Young artists would often pay for their meal with their latest canvas. Today this bohemian atmosphere has been replaced by attractive boutiques, antique stores and top-notch restaurants. ■ Where to stay ➡ 26 ■ After dark ➡ 78 ➡ 82

 # Where to eat

Torre di Pisa (12)
via Fiori Chiari 21 ☎ 02874877

Ⓜ 2 Lanza **Tuscan cuisine** ●●●● ▱ 🕓 Sept.–June Mon.–Fri., Sat. eve; July Mon.–Fri; closed Christmas–New Year's Eve, Aug.

Situated in the heart of Brera, the Torre di Pisa restaurant has been a culinary landmark and popular meeting place for around 30 years. The Meacci brothers have made the most of their limited space: customers are packed into the small rustic dining rooms and the atmosphere is both relaxed and friendly. The menu reflects the Tuscan origins of the proprietors (although they do make some concessions to Lombard dishes) and changes with the seasons ★ : spring salad with mushrooms, truffle salad in the fall… All diners are treated to an appetizer on the house. There is an excellent wine list with a bias toward Tuscan wines. Given the restaurant's size and popularity, it is best to book in advance.

Ciovassino (13)
via Ciovassino 5 ☎ 028053868

Ⓜ 1 Cairoli; 2 Lanza **Lombard and Tuscan cuisine** ●● ▱ 🕓 Mon.–Fri., Sat. eve.; closed Christmas–New Year, Aug.

Tucked away in a corner of Brera, just behind the beautiful church of Santa Maria del Carmine ➡ 99, the Ciovassino occupies the first floor of two carefully renovated 19th-century houses. The quiet atmosphere of the little cobbled street is reflected in the elegant, friendly restaurant. The Ciovassino specializes in simple, delightful cooking using seasonal ingredients. There is a good wine list. Booking is strongly advised because this restaurant attracts a lot of regular local diners as well as visitors.

Consolare (14)
via Ciovasso 4 ☎ 028053581

Ⓜ 1 Cairoli; 2 Lanza **Fish** ●●● ▱ 🕓 Tue. eve.–Sun.; closed Christmas, Aug.

Located in one of the little streets leading off piazza del Carmine, the Consolare is a modern restaurant with a young clientele and buzzing atmosphere. The menu is biased toward fish dishes, although it also features classic meat dishes such as fillet steak. ★ The giardinetto (meaning 'little garden'), an ice cream in the shape of a flower, is a popular dessert. It is advisable to book in advance.

Not forgetting

■ **Orient Express (15)** via Fiori Chiari 8 ☎ 028056227 ●●●● Relive, in the heart of Brera, the atmosphere of the legendary Orient Express in the 1920s and dine in partly reconstructed railway cars. You can eat outside in summer.
■ **Becco Rosso (16)** via San Carpoforo 7 ☎ 0286460059 ●● A light, airy restaurant serving pizzas and traditional cuisine.

What to see ➡ 98
➡ 100 Where to
shop ➡ 134

A trip through time
at the Orient
Express between
Istanbul and the
elegant Brera
district.

One of Italy's major daily newspapers, the *Corriere della Sera*, has its headquarters in via Solferino, north Brera. The adjoining streets are home to fashion stores, antique dealers and picture framers. ■ After dark ➡ 78 ■ What to see ➡ 100 ■ Where to shop ➡ 136

➡ Where to eat

La Libera (17)
via Palermo 21 ☎ 028053603

Ⓜ 2 Lanza, Moscova **Traditional Italian cuisine, pizzas** ● ▣ Ⓢ *Mon.–Fri., Sun.; closed Christmas–New Year, Aug.*

Wood paneling, old-fashioned beer advertisements, wooden chairs and glass cabinets all lend the La Libera restaurant an old Parisian bistro feel. It is frequented by a crowd of young people from the worlds of fashion and advertising. The good, original cooking includes a huge choice of salads and regional specialties such as pasta with pesto or seafood paupiettes. La Libera also serves a wide variety of delicious crusty pizzas. Always packed.

Le Bandiere (18)
via Palermo 15 ☎ 0286461646

Ⓜ 2 Lanza, Moscova **Specialties from Veneto, Trentino and Friuli** ●● ▣ Ⓢ *Mon.–Fri., Sat. evening; closed Christmas, New Year, Aug.*

Le Bandiere successfully combines culinary traditions from the Veneto, Trentino and Friuli regions of Italy. In a light and airy setting you can enjoy the restaurant's version of Venetian liver, exquisite charcuterie and meat dishes from Trentino, and delicious soups and ham from Friuli, complemented with a good wine list that features wines from the Veneto region.

Il Verdi (19)
piazza Mirabello 5 ☎ 026590797

Ⓜ 2 Moscova; 3 Turati **Traditional Italian cuisine** ● ▣ Ⓢ *Mon.–Sat.; closed Christmas–New Year, Aug. 8–30*

This successful restaurant is on the corner of the elegant piazza Mirabello. It has low lighting and simple, yet attractive decor. The menu at Il Verdi is wide-ranging and includes classic Lombard dishes (risottos, *ossobuco, cotoletta alla milanese*), traditional dishes from other regions as well as modern cuisine. There is an endless choice of salads to suit all tastes and the dessert menu is no less appealing. The staff are attentive and effecient. Very popular with those in the fashion and business world.

■ **San Fermo (20)** via San Fermo della Battaglia 1 ☎ 0229000901 ●● *Splendid restaurant serving Italian specialties and dishes that have a Spanish influence. Try turbot baked with tomatoes and olives, or beef cooked with mozzarella.*
■ **La Briciola (21)** via Solferino/via Marsala ☎ 026551012 ●●● *Family-run restaurant serving classic Milanese cuisine in a Liberty-style setting.*
■ **Rigolo (22)** largo Treves ☎ 02864 63220 ●● *Large restaurant serving regional dishes with a modern slant. Never disappoints. Good wine list and selection of grappas.*

In the area

The area around Porta Venezia is one of central Milan's green spaces. It is enhanced by the elegant neoclassical architecture of the Villa Reale ➡ 90 and by the beautiful buildings which line corso Venezia, where the city's nobility resided in the 19th century. ■ Where to stay ➡ 30

Where to eat

Joia (23)
via Panfilo Castaldi 18 ☎ 02295 22124

Ⓜ 3 Repubblica **Vegetarian cuisine** ●●● ▭ Ⓢ *Mon.–Fri, Sat eve.; closed Christmas–Jan. 6, Aug.*

This top class restaurant is managed with great flair and imagination by chef Pietro Leemann and is certainly one of the top vegetarian restaurants in Milan, if not in the whole of Italy. Delicate fish dishes are served with subtle combinations of vegetables, herbs, spices and a range of different cheeses. The desserts are just as mouth-watering. An à la carte menu is available as well as good set menus at reasonable prices. Booking is strongly advised.

Malavoglia (24)
via Lecco 4 ☎ 0229531387

Ⓜ 1 Porta Venezia **Sicilian cuisine** ●●● ▭ Ⓢ *Mon. eve–Sun.; closed Christmas, Jan. 6, Aug.*

Diners come to the Malavoglia restaurant to enjoy good Sicilian cooking and the warmth of island hospitality. In this restaurant, which is owned by the Anzalones, a family of Sicilian origin, the fish is king: dishes include spicy tuna steak, *sarde a beccafico* (sardines stuffed with pine nuts and raisins) and pasta with sardines. Also unmissable are the sublime cassata (ice cream containing nuts and candied fruit) and the delectable fig pie. Try the prickly pears when they are in season. Booking is essential.

Rosy e Gabriele (25)
via Sirtori 26 ☎ 0229525930

Ⓜ 1 Porta Venezia **Mediterranean cuisine, pizzas** ●● ▭ Ⓢ *Mon.–Tue., Thur.–Sun.; closed Christmas, Aug.*

Next door to the Diana Majestic Hotel ➡ 31, the Rosy e Gabriele is a busy, popular restaurant that has long been the area's main trattoria. As you enter you are greeted with an aquarium of live lobsters and an array of freshly-caught fish arranged on a glass counter. For a light lunch try the warm and cold salads; for something a bit more substantial try the excellent Mediterranean meat and the choice of fish dishes will not disappoint. Good range of pizzas. The service is fast and efficient. The restaurant stays open late and all the dishes remain available.

Not forgetting

■ **Lucca (26)** via Panfilo Castaldi 33 ☎ 0229526668 ●● *Excellent traditional Tuscan cuisine. 1950s ambience with period furniture. Good value for money.*

■ **Il Transatlantico (27)** via Malpighi 3 ☎ 0229526098 ● *Housed in one of the city's most beautiful Liberty-style buildings, decorated with attractive majolica pottery, this pizzeria serves excellent classic cuisine. Tables outside in the summer.*

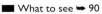

■ What to see ➡ 90

23

A short walk from Porta Venezia,
a magnificent Liberty-style *palazzo*
houses the pizzeria Il Transatlantico.

24

27

25

The area around Stazione Centrale, at one time the main entry point into Milan, is dotted with numerous hotels and restaurants. Nearby is another railway station, Stazione Garibaldi. The whole area is criss-crossed with busy streets and is pleasant to stroll around. The numerous

Where to eat

Cavallini (28)
via Mauro Macchi 2 ☎ 026693771

Ⓜ 2 Centrale F.S.; 3 Centrale F.S. **Classic cuisine** ●● ▯ Ⓞ *Mon.–Fri.; closed Christmas, Aug.* ❤ *Il Vigneto (also has a separate wine bar)*

In the early 1930s Settimo Cavallini took over the ownership of Trattoria Fiorentina and rechristened it. Today, the Cavallini restaurant serves both classic cuisine and a range of more experimental dishes. There is an excellent wine list. You can also enjoy a glass of wine in the adjoining bar, Il Vigneto.

Hong Kong (29)
via Schiaparelli 5 ☎ 0267071790

Ⓜ 2 Centrale F.S.; 3 Centrale F.S. **Chinese cuisine** ●● ▯ Ⓞ *Tue.–Sun.*

Milan's most elegant Chinese restaurant, the Hong Kong, is attractively decorated, but surprisingly not in Chinese style. Beautifully presented tables are laid with silver cutlery. The elaborate and imaginatively served Canton and Sichuan dishes are quite exquisite and are beautifully presented. Service is fast and unobtrusive.

Osteria del Treno (30)
via San Gregorio 46-48 ☎ 02670 0479

Ⓜ 2 Centrale F.S.; 3 Centrale F.S. **Lombard cuisine** ●● ▱ Ⓞ *Mon.–Fri, Sun.; closed Christmas–New Year, Easter, Aug.*

This atmospheric restaurant near to the station actually used to be a railroad workers' club. It still has the old smoke-filled atmosphere of a traditional *osteria* (tavern) about it. The place is buzzing and noisy; the service is simple and courteous; the tasty food is inspired by Mantovan traditions: there is an impressive choice of dishes that feature sausages and ham. ★ Try the tortelli with courgette and *salamella* (sausage in the shape of a horseshoe). There is a good wine list.

Caffè India (31)
via Petrella 19 ☎ 0229405870

Ⓜ 1 Lima **Indian cuisine** ● ▯ Ⓞ *Tue.–Sun.; closed New Year–Jan. 6, Easter, Aug.*

A warm welcome greets diners in this richly decorated Indian restaurant where a relaxed atmosphere prevails. Fresh ingredients and subtle blends of spices combine to produce a range of sumptuous dishes. The menu features all the classic chicken, lamb and fish curries and a number of tandoori dishes. Good value for money.

Not forgetting

■ **Centro ittico (32)** via Ferrante Aporti 35 ☎ 02261 43774 ●●●●
Choose your fish from one of Milan's best-known fish stalls, and then it is cooked and prepared for you in a bright, 'nautical' setting.

international restaurants
reflect the cosmopolitan
character of this area
■ Where to stay ➡ 32

In the area

The Centro direzionale, near Stazione Garibaldi, is soon to become the city's administrative center. Restaurants have multiplied in the area, catering for a business clientele at midday, and a more varied crowd in the evening. The places below are worth checking out.

 # Where to eat

Porção (33)
via Abbadesse 30 ☎ 026883883

M 2 Gioia; 3 Sondrio **Brazilian cuisine** ●●● ▭ 🕐 *Mon.–Sat.; closed Christmas, New Year*

Porção presents a real surprise to diners: a traditional Lombard farmhouse, (which has resisted all creeping urbanization) where you really feel as if you are suddenly in the country, is the setting for this very busy, fun Brazilian restaurant. Porção offers an excellent choice of appetizers and its specialty is dishes which feature spit-roast meat. Everything in the restaurant is designed to create an authentic Brazilian atmosphere: warm decor, brightly colored flowers and tropical fruit. But before you eat anything, set yourself up for the evening with a caipirinha aperitif!

Berti (34)
via Algarotti 20 ☎ 026694627

M 2 Gioia **Lombard cuisine** ● ▭ 🕐 *Mon.–Sat.; closed Christmas–Jan. 6, Aug.*

Berti is situated at the end of a cul-de-sac which is bordered with pretty gardens, on the first floor of an old apartment block. Large and welcoming, the restaurant serves fine Lombard cuisine that is lovingly prepared and served in the traditional way. The service is friendly.
★ In summer diners can escape the heat of the city by sitting outside in a large shady garden. The wine list is exceptional and features all the best Italian wines.

Langhe (35)
corso Como 6 ☎ 02655 4279

M 2 Garibaldi F.S. **Piedmontese cuisine from the Langhe** ●● ▭ 🕐 *Mon.–Sat.; closed Christmas–Jan. 6, Aug.*

The Langhe region is in south Piedmont, the area that produces such famous wines as barolo, barbaresco, nebbiolo and dolcetto. All of these can be sampled in this restaurant as an accompaniment to the excellent cuisine. Among the most mouth-watering specialties on offer are braised meats, beef carpaccio, *agnolotti* (pasta stuffed with meat), mushrooms and the exquisite Alba white truffle dish. The wooden decor creates an old Piedmont feel. The Langhe is frequented by gourmets and connoisseurs of Piedmontese cuisine. There is an excellent wine list.

Not forgetting

■ **Sushi bar Mino (36)** via Adda ☎ 02670 2539 ●● *A little corner of Japan. Excellent sushi served at affordable prices.*
■ **Al Garibaldi (37)** viale Monte Grappa 7 ☎ 02659 8006 ●●● *Milanese cuisine complemented by a good wine list, all served in a really comfortable setting.*
■ **Aquila d'oro (38)** via Carlo Farini 31 ☎ 02608 0703 ● *An old-style restaurant with very good service, that serves first class traditional Tuscan cuisine.*

■ After dark
➡ 76 ➡ 80
■ Where to shop
➡ 138

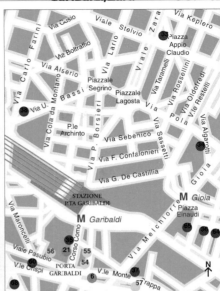

Via Keplero
Via Cusio
Viale Stelvio
Piazza
Appio
Claudio
Via Carlo Farini
Via Boltraffio
Via Alserio
Via Lario
Viale Zara
Via Taramelli
Via Rossellini
Via Oldofredi
Viale Restelli
Piazzale Segrino
Via Cola da Montano
Via Bassi
Piazzale Lagosta
Via U.
Via P. Borsieri
Pola
Via Algarotti
P.le Archinto
Via Sebenico
Via Sassetti
Via F. Confalonieri
Via G. De Castillia
Gioia
STAZIONE P.TA GARIBALDI
M Garibaldi
Via Melchiorre
M Gioia
Piazza Einaudi
Via Maroncelli
Viale Pasubio
Corso Como
56 21 55
54
N
V.le Crispi
PORTA GARIBALDI
6
V.le Monte
57 Trappa

The cellars of Milanese restaurants offer the best regional and national wines.

In the area

The streets around via Paolo Sarpi are full of stores selling goods at the cheaper end of the scale. Nearby there is a mini-Chinatown where leather goods stalls, Chinese supermarkets and restaurants do a flourishing trade. The atmosphere is lively and bustling, especially on Saturdays.

Where to eat

Il Sambuco (39)
via Messina 10 ☎ 0233610333

🔲 12, 14, 29, 30 **Fish dishes** ●●●● ▣ 🕔 *Mon.–Fri., Sat. eve.: closed Christmas–New Year, Easter, Aug.*

The city of Milan can claim with some justification to be the 'mainland capital' of Italian fish cuisine, thanks to its large market and celebrity chefs. Set in elegant, genteel, plush surroundings, Il Sambuco, which is the restaurant of the Hermitage hotel ➡ 34, is without doubt the place to go for seafood. ★ The fish and seafood dishes are prepared with great imagination and flair. The meat dishes are also excellent and there is a mouth-watering selection of desserts to choose from. Although the restaurant is fairly large, it is essential to book in advance to avoid disappointment as it is very popular. There is a good selection of affordable wines.

Vecchio Porco (40)
via Messina 8 ☎ 02313862

🔲 12, 14, 29, 30 **Traditional Italian cuisine** ●● ▣ 🕔 *Tue.–Sat., Sun. eve.; closed Christmas–Jan. 6, Easter, Aug.*

At the Vecchio Porco, the pig, as the restaurant's name suggests, is king: there are pig posters and photographs on the walls and even pig ceramics and statues in the many windows. In warmer weather diners can sit outside on a large terrace. The restaurant, which is situated very near to the Hermitage hotel, serves classic cuisine as well as pizzas, ranging from the traditional to the more inventive Vecchio Porco specialities. The clientele is young and lively. As this is a rather trendy place to dine, reservations are strongly recommended.

Pechino (41)
via Cenisio 7 ☎ 0233101668

🔲 12, 14 **Chinese cuisine** ●●● ▣ 🕔 *Tue.–Sun.; closed Christmas–New Year, Jul. 15–Aug. 15*

One of Milan's top Chinese restaurants, as well as one of the first to be established in the city, the Pechino is small, intimate and attractively decorated with flowers and traditional Chinese ornaments. The relaxed cozy atmosphere and the warm welcome of the owner, Pan-I-Sceng, will soon make you feel relaxed and at home. Born in Milan of Chinese parents, Pan-I-Sceng speaks fluent Chinese, Italian and, of course, Milanese dialect! The Beijing-style food is well presented, delicate and full of flavor.

Not forgetting

■ **La Torre del Mangia (42)** via Procaccini 37 ☎ 02314871 ●●
Traditional Tuscan cuisine with an emphasis on fish dishes. Lively, bustling atmosphere.

■ Where to stay ➥ 34

Map of Sarpi district showing streets:
Piazza Diocleziano, Via Gran S. Bernardo, Via Losanna, Via Borgese, Via L. Castelvetro, Via F.lli Induno, Via Cenisio, Piazza Gerusalemme, Via Tartaglia, Via Monviso, Via Paolo, Via Messina, Via Luigi Nono, Via G.B. Bertini, Via Procaccini, Via Lomazzo, Via Aleardi, Via Paolo, Via A. Fioravanti, Via Giordano Bruno, Via Sarpi, Via Bramante, Via G. Giusti

39

39

101 specialties from the fish dishes at Il Sambuco to the pork at Vecchio Porco.

40

VECCHIO E BELL PORCO E MEGLI

40

40

41

41

In the area

One of Napoleon's grand projects was to make corso Sempione into a highway linking the Arco della Pace ➡ 99 and the Arc de Triomphe in Paris. This grand avenue leads to Milan's biggest park, Parco Sempione ➡ 99. Hotels and restaurants have mushroomed in the area owing to its

Where to eat

Taverna della Trisa (43)
via Ferruccio 1 ☎ 02341304

🚇 1, 19, 27, 57, 94 **Trentino cuisine** ●● 🔲 🕙 *Tue.–Sat., 1 Sun. out of 2; closed Christmas–New Year, Aug.*

With its rustic, cozy atmosphere and dark wooden furniture, the Taverna della Trisa has something of a mountain retreat feel to it. In warmer weather you can counter this wintry feel by sitting out in the restaurant's shady garden. The cooking, from the Trentino region, is full of flavor: the meat- and venison-based winter dishes are slightly modified and lightened in the summer months. The wine list features many wines from the Trentino-Alto Adige region, including such superior white wines as lagrein, teroldego and riesling, and fragrant reds from Lake Caldaro. ★ After your dessert try the grappa, the local brandy or the colorless spirits also produced in the Trentino.

Arrow's (44)
via Mantegna 17–19 ☎ 02341533

🚇 1, 19, 29, 57, 94 **Fish specialties** ●●● 🔲 🕙 *Mon.–Sat.; closed Christmas–New Year, Aug.* 🔳

Those wishing to dine at Arrow's restaurant are advised to book well in advance. The restaurant is light and airy despite the fact that it is not very large (it holds about 30 diners). This family-run establishment has a widespread reputation and people often come from far afield to sample its excellent range of fish dishes. Seafood, pasta dishes, white fish (depending on the catch and always very fresh) are cooked with great care and delicacy. The young staff are attentive and efficient.

Osteria della Cagnola (45)
via Cirillo 14 ☎ 023319428

🚇 1, 29, 30 **Lombard and traditional Italian cuisine** ●●● 🔲 🕙 *Mon.–Sat.; closed Christmas–Epiphany, Aug.*

Near the Arco della Pace ➡ 99, this restaurant run by Roberto Facchini is very popular with connoisseurs and gourmets. The small dining room has a warm, homey feel. The menu features a range of stylish dishes. There is a good choice of pasta (*primi*), as well as meat and fish dishes (*secondi*). There is also a tempting dessert menu; worth trying are the fruit pies, which melt in your mouth. The service is impeccable and extremely courteous. Booking is essential given the small size of the restaurant.

Not forgetting

■ **Le Pietre Cavate (46)** via Castelvetro 14 ☎ 02344704 ●●●●
A warm, welcoming restaurant serving good Tuscan cuisine prepared with fresh seasonal ingredients.
■ **Gino e Franco (47)** largo Domodossola 2 ☎ 02312003 ●●
Traditional, classic cuisine. Pleasant outside seating area in warm weather.
■ **Montecristo (48)** via Prina 17 ☎ 02312 760 ●●●● *Top-class cuisine (mainly fish dishes) in a bright, elegant setting.*

proximity to the Fiera.
■ Where to stay
➡ 34 ■ What to see
➡ 98

After a pleasant walk in
Parco Sempione, enjoy
a meal in one of corso
Sempione's fine restaurants.

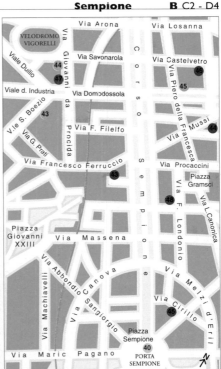

44

43

43

45

47

45

In the area

River Ticino feeds Milan's navigable canals and flows into the city's docks, the Darsena ➡ 94. The public housing blocks and warehouses in this area are a remnant from 19th-century Milan's industrial past. Restaurants, bars and *birrerie* (beer bars) abound. ■ What to see ➡ 94

# Where to eat

Sadler (49)
via Conchetta/via Troilo 14 ☎ 0258104451

▦ 3, 15, 59 **Modern cuisine** ●●●●● ▱ ◷ *Mon.–Sat. eves only; closed Jan., Aug.*

Despite his youth, Claudio Sadler has already accumulated a wealth of experience, placing him firmly at the cutting edge of Milanese cuisine. First impressions on entering his new restaurant near the Pavese canal are of a pervading elegance, which bodes well for the food to follow. The cuisine is truly creative and experimental and matches unusual flavors. The menu changes frequently, proof of Sadler's passion for the new. You'll be spoiled for choice with the set menus and the *à la carte* dishes. The quality of wines in the cellar matches the high standards of the rest of the restaurant. Booking is essential.

Il Montalcino (50)
via Valenza 17 ☎ 0289403783

Ⓜ 2 Porta Genova F.S. **Tuscan cuisine** ●●● ▱ ◷ *Mon.–Sat. eves only; closed New Year and for some of Aug.*

Dining out at the Montalcino, a little corner of Tuscany overlooking the Naviglio Grande canal, is an unmissable experience. Marta Sandoli now runs this family restaurant and, in good Tuscan tradition, continues to serve as accompaniments to her classic cooking the legendary heady brunello and the nobile rosso, both from Montalcino, as well as several well-known white wines. Everything here is reminiscent of central Tuscany. Specialties include game, venison and red meats. Booking is advisable.

Al Porto (51)
piazza Cantore (previously casello daziario) ☎ 028321481

▦ 2, 9, 14, 20, 29, 47, 59, 74 **Fish restaurant** ●●●● ▱ ◷ *Mon. eve.–Sat.; closed Christmas–New Year, Aug.*

Up until World War I there were toll gates at every entry point to the city; here taxes were levied on all merchandise entering the town. One of these toll houses, at Porta Genova, is now the venue for one of Milan's most popular fish restaurants. ★ The lovely garden overlooking the Darsena docks ➡ 94 provides further seating capacity. Given the popularity of this restaurant, reservations are advisable.

Not forgetting

■ **Osteria del Binari (52)** via Tortona 1 ☎ 0289406753 ●● *Located behind Porta Genova station, this is an elegant and stylish restaurant with a lovely garden in summer.*
■ **Osteria di via Prè (53)** via Casale 4 ☎ 028373869 ●●●
Next to Porta Genova station, this restaurant specializes in Ligurian dishes and wines.
■ **Asso di Fiori Osteria dei Formaggi (54)** alzaia Naviglio Grande 54 ☎ 0289409415 ● *Cheese and good wines, complemented by an enormous selection of bread and flavored oils.*

■ Where to shop
➜ 142 ➜ 144

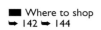

50

50

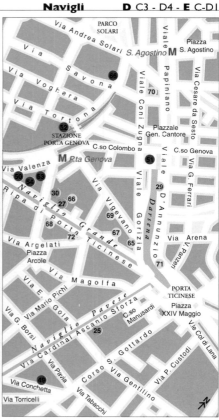

PARCO SOLARI

Via Andrea Solari

S. Agostino **M** Piazza S. Agostino

Via Savona

Via

Via Voghera

Via Tortona

Viale Coni Zugna

Viale Papiniano

Via Cesare da Sesto

66

70

STAZIONE PORTA GENOVA

C.so Colombo

Piazzale Gen. Cantore

C.so Genova

M *Pta Genova*

61

Via Valenza

50 52 53

Naviglio Grande

Ripa di Porta Ticinese

30

27

66

68

72

Via Vigevano

69

67

65

Viale Gorizia

Darsena

Viale D'Annunzio

Via G. Ferrari

29

Via Arena V. Panzieri

71

Via Argelati

Piazza Arcole

Via Magolfa

PORTA TICINESE

Piazza XXIV Maggio

Via E. Gola

Via Mario Pichi

Via G. Borsi

Naviglio Pavese

Via Cardinal Ascanio Sforza

C.so Manusardi

25

V.le Col di Lana

Via Pavia

Corso S. Gottardo

Via Gentilino

Via P. Custodi

Via Conchetta

48

Via Torricelli

Via Tabacchi

51

51

Rustic restaurants line the banks of Milan's *navigli* (canals).

49

53

51

In the area

Between Porta Ticinese ➡ 94 and Porta Romana in the south there are a number of beautiful churches (Sant'Eustorgio, San Lorenzo Maggiore ➡ 94, San Nazaro Maggiore ➡ 92). Elegant town houses line the corso Italia and corso di Porta Romana. ■ Where to stay ➡ 20 ➡ 22

Where to eat

Ulmet (55)
via Disciplini / via Olmetto ☎ 0286452718

▣ 15, 65 **Modern cuisine** ●●●●● ▢ 🕐 *Mon. eve.–Sat.; closed Christmas–Jan. 6, Aug.*

Housed in the first floor of an old *palazzo* in the shadow of San Lorenzo Maggiore basilica ➡ 94, the Ulmet restaurant offers a charming historic setting in which to eat – coffered ceilings, a large fireplace where a roaring fire blazes in winter, period furniture, attractively laid tables, silver and crystal glasses. The cuisine mixes Lombard tradition with innovation: try the pheasant mousse, ravioli filled with turbot or lobster bisque, and, for dessert, try fruits of the forest in puff pastry with lemon cream au gratin. This is first class cuisine, sometimes with a nouvelle cuisine touch, but never forgetting its rural origins. The clientele is fashionable and wealthy, and partly made up of local business diners. The dining room is small, so booking is advisable.

Alla Collina Pistoiese (56)
via Amedei 1 ☎ 0286451085

▣ 15, 65 **Tuscan cuisine** ●●● ▢ 🕐 *Mon.–Thur., Sat. eve–Sun.; closed Christmas–New Year, Easter, week of Aug. 15*

The Collina Pistoiese, which is located in a pedestrianized area near piazza Sant'Alessandro, has been serving the city's best Tuscan specialties in a huge wood-paneled dining room since 1938. Its regular customers, including a number of celebrities, come here for its authentic, rich Tuscan cuisine.

Yar (57)
via Giuseppe Mercalli 22 ☎ 0258305234

▣ 15, 65, 94 **Russian cuisine** ●●●● ▢ 🕐 *eves. only, Mon.–Sat.; closed Christmas, New Year*

Step through the door of the Yar and you find yourself in another world. The samovar, the columns covered in birch, the red velvet furnishings and the ceilings decorated with oriental frescos transport you to a literary, timeless Russia. Next to the formal, luxurious dining room, the more modest bistro gives you a chance to try dishes at a more competitive price. ★ Among the highlights on the menu, served in both rooms, are different varieties of caviar and smoked fish (sturgeon and salmon), flavored with aromatic herbs. The meat dishes are also appealing (try the lamb, or the chicken with blueberries). The typically Nordic desserts are hearty and full of flavor. The vodka should be drunk in the traditional Russian manner – ice cold!

Not forgetting

■ **La Dolce Vita (58)** via Bergamini 11 ☎ 0258303843 ●● *Traditional Italian cuisine. La Dolce Vita offers candlelit dinners, served in an elegant, colonnaded dining room, to the sounds of relaxing piano music.*

After dark ➡ 76
What to see ➡ 92

55

57

56

Bread flavored with salt, olive oil, garlic and rosemary and other Tuscan specialties at the Collina Pistoiese.

56

55

57

Basic facts

Many cookery writers have dwelt on the rich tradition of Milanese cooking. It is founded on three pillars: saffron risotto (*risotto giallo*) with its warm appetizing color, *ossobuco* served with *gremolata* (a sauce made of tomatoes, anchovies and zest of lemon) and the *cotoletta alla milanese*

Where to eat

Alfredo Gran San Bernardo (59)
via Borgese 14 ☎ 023319000

📷 *12, 14* **Traditional Milanese cuisine** ●●●●● 💳 🕐 *Jan.–May: Mon.–Sat.; June–July: Mon.–Fri.; closed Christmas–Jan. 6, Aug.*

Alfredo Valli is a master of Lombard and Milanese cuisine. Though a little way out of the center of the city, his restaurant is first class and very elegant. The small dining rooms with wood-paneling and low lighting are both comfortable and welcoming. The menu combines traditional dishes with international cuisine. The wine list is of the same high standard.

Antica Trattoria della Pesa (60)
viale Pasubio 10 ☎ 026555741

📷 *94* **Milanese cuisine** ●●● 💳 🕐 *Mon.–Sat.; closed Christmas–New Year, Aug.*

In front of the Antica Trattoria della Pesa in viale Pasubio, which at one time ran alongside the outer city walls, you can still see the iron platform which was once used to weigh carts laden with merchandise to determine how much toll they should pay. The trattoria dates back to this period, but today, in the hands of Delio Sassi, it is a top restaurant with first class service. However, some of the old-style atmosphere remains.

Masuelli Trattoria San Marco (61)
viale Umbria 80 ☎ 0255184138

📷 *12, 27, 92* **Lombard and Piedmontese cuisine** ●● 💳 🕐 *Mon. eve.–Sat.; closed Christmas–Jan. 6, Aug. 15–Sep. 15*

For three generations the Masuelli family have been running the San Marco on viale Umbria. It is a simple restaurant, offering quality cooking. The decor is traditional, the atmosphere friendly. Giuseppe (Pinuccio to his friends) reels off the menu with aplomb. It's also worth following his advice on which wines to choose.

Trattoria Milanese (62)
via Santa Marta 11 ☎ 0286451991

Ⓜ *1 Cordusio* **Milanese and Lombard cuisine** ●● 💳 🕐 *Mon., Wed.–Sun.; closed Christmas–Jan. 6, Aug.*

In this little restaurant, consisting of two rooms, one more formal and the other more relaxed and cozy, the Villa familly have been serving authentic Milanese cooking since 1919. Giuseppe looks after his large clientele of regulars with consumate skill and welcomes casual customers, who come in ever-increasing numbers, with a smile. Book ahead to avoid disappointment.

Not forgetting

■ **La Nôs (63)** via Bramante 35 ☎ 02331 5363 ●●● *Traditional cuisine. Excellent service. Good set menus.*

(veal chops) of
Austrian origin.

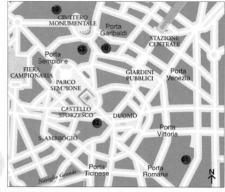

Ossobuco with *risotto
giallo* (saffron rice): a well-
known Lombard specialty.

Foreign cuisine has really taken off in Milan. The trend started in the small Chinatown district around via Canonica and was followed by Greek, Indian and Mexican restaurants. Japanese restaurants offering sushi and sashimi are the latest arrivals on the scene.

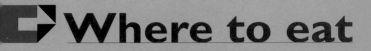

➡ Where to eat

Taiwan (64)
via Adda 10 ☎ 02670 2488

🅼 2 Gioia **Taiwanese cuisine** ● 🔳 🕒 *Wed.–Mon., closed Christmas, New Year*

The subtle fragrances of Taiwanese cooking, much less familiar than its Cantonese neighbor, are on offer here. The decor is quite un-Chinese: the walls are in pastel shades and the furnishings are simple and minimalist, almost Japanese. The food is a real treat for the palate: besides the better-known dishes there are some more unusual dishes such as steamed chicken bun or fragrant rice served in bamboo.

Ran (65)
via Bordoni 8/10 ☎ 026696997

🅼 2 Gioia **Japanese cuisine** ●●● 🔳 🕒 *Mon.–Sat. eves only; closed Aug.*

Japanese food in Milan is generally very expensive. However, in this restaurant the sushi, sashimi, tempura and other chicken, vegetable or fish-based dishes are more affordable. The restaurant is always full of Japanese. It is well-lit and the decor is pleasant and simple, with light wood paneling and black tables. Staff, dressed in kimonos, are attentive and helpful.

Joe Peña's (66)
via Savona 17 ☎ 0258110820

🚋 14, 29, 30, 68 **Mexican cuisine** ● 🔳 🕒 *Tue.–Fri., Sat. eve–Sun.; closed Christmas, week of Aug. 15*

Mexican restaurants have become very popular in Milan, more for their warm atmosphere, their drinks (tequila, beer with lime), and their famous chili con carne

65

66   65   64

than for the quality of their cuisine. The atmosphere is fun and bustling; portions are generous and the list of cocktails is impressive. A good night out.

Mikonos (67)
via Tofane 5 ☎ 02261 0209

M / Gorla **Greek cuisine** ● 🍴 🕐 *eves. only: Mon., Wed.–Sun.; closed Christmas, New Year, Aug.*

This little corner of Greece has found refuge in an old Milanese house where viale Monza meets the Martesana Canal. As its name suggests, the restaurant specializes in dishes from the Cyclades islands, but also serves traditional dolmades, souvlaki, tzatziki, taramasalata and moussaka, washed down with retsina. The restaurant is very popular and always full; there are even two sittings, one at 8.30pm, the other at 10.30pm. Friendly, efficient service. Booking is advisable.

Not forgetting

Serendib (68) via Pontida 2 ☎ 02659 2139 ● *Sri Lankan cuisine served with elegance amid burnished copper and ebony wood.*

Basic facts

Although the pizza originated in Naples, it is impossible to talk about restaurants in Milan without mentioning pizzerias. The pizza chefs invent new toppings every day. Service is swift, the setting is cheerful and bright, the clientele young and lively. Eating at a pizzeria is a practical

Where to eat

Di Gennaro (69)
via Santa Radegonda 14 ☎ 028053454

M / Duomo; 3 Duomo **Pizzeria** ● ▭ ◐ Mon.–Wed., Fri.–Sun.

This is the finest of Milan's pizzerias. Located between Rinascente ➡ 120, the Duomo ➡ 86 and the Galleria Vittorio Emanuele II ➡ 86, this pizzeria is always full, especially after the late night movie showing. As well as the classic pizzas, it offers focaccia, and you can choose your own topping.

Be Bop (70)
viale Col di Lana 4 ☎ 028376972

▣ 9, 15, 29, 30 **Pizzeria** ● ▭ ◐ Tue.–Sun.

The Be Bop menu has some unusual offerings. The pizza bases are made with wholemeal flour or soya. Each month there are new toppings depending on the inspiration of the *pizzaiolo* (pizza chef): pizza with gorgonzola and pears or 'white' pizza with vegetable purée.

Charleston (71)
piazza Liberty 8 ☎ 02798631

M / Duomo; 3 Duomo **Pizzeria** ● ▱ ◐ Tue.–Sun.; closed Aug.

Centrally located near offices and movie theaters, this pizzeria is always packed. Swift service. Varied menu. Besides pizzas, the Charleston has a big self-service buffet and also serves some classic dishes.

Pizza Big (72)
viale Brianza 30 ☎ 022846548

M / Loreto; 2 Loreto **Pizzeria** ● ▱ ◐ Mon.–Sat.; closed Christmas, New Year, Aug.

Large, thin, crusty pizzas with good toppings, served at top speed by young waiting staff. The menu boasts more than 70 pizzas. Some, such as the curry pizza and the sweet coconut pizza, are interesting and a little out of the ordinary.

La Pizzaccia (73)
via don Bosco 11 ☎ 025692094

M 3 Lodi **Pizzeria** ● ▭ ◐ Tue.–Sat.; closed New Year, Aug.

A rustic, bustling pizzeria where tender, tasty pizzas are served on wooden plates. Meat dishes, vegetables and salads are also served. Always packed.

Not forgetting

■ **Premiata Pizzeria (74)** via De Amicis 22 ☎ 0289406075
● *Large pizzeria with stylish furnishings. Tables on the terrace in summer. Besides pizzas and focaccia, classic dishes are also available.*
■ **Happiness (75)** via Ravizza 4 ☎ 024814295 ● *Imaginative pizzas*

option if you are in
a hurry and is one
of the cheapest
meals out.

69

70

71

72

The pizza chef kneads the dough on
the floured marble surface and throws
it around until it gets bigger, thinner and
finally forms a perfect round!

73

73

After dark

Nightlife
Brera and Navigli are among
Milan's most charming districts
and liveliest nightspots, buzzing
with bars and jazz clubs. There
are some dance clubs here too,
but most tend to be a little way
out of the center.

Buying tickets in advance

You can buy tickets for shows, plays and concerts from:
La Biglietteria corso Garibaldi 81 ☎ 026598956
Music Tour piazzale Cadorna (in the Ferrovie Nord station) ☎ 02865578
A commission of 10% is charged.

Nights out

THE INSIDER'S FAVORITES

Movies in English

Movies in English are shown regularly at the following:

Anteo *in the center, via Milazzo 9*
☎ 026597732

Arcobaleno
near Porta Venezia, viale Tunisia 11
☎ 0229406054

Mexico *in the Navigli district, via Savona 57* ☎ 0248951802

Milan in summer

There is plenty going on between June and September in Milan: theater, movie festivals, jazz, pop and rock concerts, and international music festivals. The summer program of events changes every year. Information is available from:

Centro servizi del Comune
Galleria Vittorio Emanuele II
☎ 0262083101
🕐 *Mon.–Sat. 8.30am–7pm*

Music lovers associate Milan with one of the world's greatest opera houses, La Scala ➥ 88. Those who like symphonic and chamber music can enjoy concerts at the Conservatorio, the city's most prestigious music school, founded in 1807.

After dark

Teatro alla Scala (1)
piazza della Scala ☎ 0272003744

Ⓜ *1 Duomo; 3 Duomo* 🕐 *times vary* ● *prices vary* ▤ *Reservations by phone (24 hr line, tickets limited to two per call) residents* ☎ 02860775; *non-residents* ☎ 02860787; *over-65s* ☎ 02860863/ *confirmation by fax* ➠ 028717781/Infotel Scala ☎ 0272003744 (10am–6pm)

For opera buffs and lovers of classical music a trip to Milan must include a visit to this most famous of the world's opera houses. La Scala was inaugurated in 1778 with *Europa Riconosciuta* by the composer Antonio Salieri and soon became famous throughout the world for its excellent acoustics and for its very exacting audiences. La Scala often determines the success or failure of an opera. Not even great composers have been exempt: Rossini, Donizetti, Bellini, Verdi and Puccini all had to submit their premieres to the scrutiny of La Scala audiences. La Scala established itself on the international scene with the arrival of Arturo Toscanini in 1901. After the building was destroyed in World War 11, a rapid rebuilding program was carried out. Its reopening under the baton of its great conductor, Toscanini, on May 11, 1946, after just one year of building work, was an amazing achievement. In the post-war years, Claudio Abbado, Carlo Maria Giulini and the great soprano Maria Callas all enjoyed moments of glory here. Today it is owned by the city and is under the musical direction of Riccardo Muti. The season consists of opera and ballets and also includes a variety of classical and chamber music concerts and song recitals. The theater has 2000 seats divided between the orchestra, four tiers of balconies and two galleries. You can buy tickets or get information on how to book at the box office in via Filodrammatici. Tickets are strictly limited to two per person.

Conservatorio (2)
via Conservatorio 12 ☎ 027621101

▦ *9, 12, 23, 29, 30, 54, 61, 94* 🕐 *times vary* ● *prices vary*

The Giuseppe Verdi Conservatorio has two concert halls and hosts concerts covering the symphonic repertoire as well as chamber music. The sala Verdi is able to seat an audience of 1500. It hosts afternoon and evening concerts and attracts world-class performers. The Giuseppe Verdi symphony orchestra also plays here regularly. The smaller sala Puccini, with 400 seats, hosts numerous concerts throughout the year and sometimes ballets are performed here. Tickets can be bought at the Conservatorio box office just before the performance or at the numerous ticket offices in the city.

■ **San Maurizio al Monastero Maggiore (3)** via Luini 2 ☎ 02877532 *In spring and autumn the church hosts the San Maurizio Festival of Music and Poetry, featuring early music concerts given by musicians of international renown performing on period instruments. Interesting and unusual performances.*

Piazza della Scala hosts many big events. December 7 is the opening gala of the La Scala season and the festival of Saint Ambrose, patron saint of Milan.

The number of theaters in the city testifies to the Milanese love of the dramatic art. You can see plays ranging from the classic to the avant-garde, plays in Lombard dialect, operetta, contemporary dance and variety shows.

After dark

Piccolo Teatro (4)
via Rovello 2 ☎ 02723331

M / *Cordusio* ◐ *times vary* ● *prices vary*

Nina Vinchi, Paolo Grassi and Giorgio Strehler are the founders of one of Europe's most important civic theaters. Located in via Rovello since 1947, the Piccolo Teatro made its name with its staging of plays by Bertolt Brecht and numerous works at the cutting edge of contemporary theater. Over the years it has widened its repertoire while still maintaining rigorously high standards. The Piccolo also manages two other theaters in the city (same telephone number for all three theaters): the Teatro Studio (via Rivoli 6), formerly Teatro Fossati, which was first set up as a rehearsal space before becoming a theater in its own right, and the Piccolo Teatro (largo Greppi), a new building with an auditorium seating 1,200, designed by architect Marco Zanusso and finally opened in 1998.

Teatro Lirico (5)
via Larga 14 ☎ 02809665

M / *Duomo; 3 Duomo, Missori* ◐ *times vary* ● *prices vary*

Founded in the late 19th century, the Teatro Lirico has a seating capacity of 1,800 which allows it to stage large-scale works. The Lirico theater concentrates largely on works by Italian playwrights but it also stages some popular and successful foreign productions, concerts and spectacular dance shows. Since 1998 the Lirico has been under the management of the Giuseppe Verdi Symphony Orchestra.

Entertainment, from variety shows to rock concerts, from dance to classical theater.

Teatro Smeraldo (6)
piazza XXV Aprile ☎ 0229006767

Ⓜ 2 Garibaldi ◐ times vary ● prices vary

Established in the 1940s, the Teatro Smeraldo is the city's largest theater with a seating capacity of 2000. The city's main dance forum, it is also the only venue for variety shows.

Teatro Nazionale (7)
piazza Piemonte 12 ☎ 0248007700

🚃 18, 24, 61, 63, 67 ◐ times vary ● prices vary

Founded in 1924, transformed into a movie theater and then back to a theater at the end of the 1970s, the Teatro Nazionale can seat 1600. It stages classics from the Italian repertoire, operettas, ballets and concerts.

Not forgetting

▬ **Palavobis (8)** via Sant'Elia 33 ☎ 0233400551 *Stages operettas.*
▬ **Teatro Carcano (9)** corso di Porta Romana 65 ☎ 0255181377 *Stages plays, especially by Milanese writers.*

Basic facts

Night-owls will be spoiled for choice when it comes to deciding in which bar to end the evening. Whether you are looking for a piece of history, a piano bar, live music, or young, trendy bars full of artists or top models, there is something to suit all tastes…

After dark

Café L'Atlantique (10)
viale Umbria 42 ☎ 0255193925

🚋 12, 27, 92 🕐 Tue.–Fri. 9pm–3am, Sun. noon–4pm; closed Aug. ● **Show** price varies 🏨

Located in the south of the city, Café l'Atlantique is the fashionable place to be seen. This vast complex comprises a bar, a wine bar and a restaurant which serves food until 1am. The decor is futurist and minimalist, the clientele consists mainly of top models, designers and advertising executives. ★ An exclusive setting for Sunday brunch.

Bar Giamaica (11)
via Brera 32 ☎ 02876723

🚋 3, 4, 12, 61, 73 🕐 daily. 9–2am; closed week of Aug. 15 ● prices vary

Bar Giamaica was established in 1921 and is a short walk away from the Pinacoteca di Brera ➡ 100. In the 1960s it quickly became the haunt of painters, intellectuals and 'rebels'. Today it attracts a young crowd, top models and advertising executives, but still retains something of its former bohemian atmosphere. It is very pleasant in summer when you can sit outdoors in the garden.

Bar Magenta (12)
via Carducci 13 ☎ 028053808

🚋 18, 19, 20, 24, 94 🕐 Tue.–Sun. 7.30–3am ● prices vary

Bar Magenta is one of Milan's oldest bars. The decor dates from the early 20th century. Beer, hot food and sandwiches are served till late. The Music ranges from techno and house to rock. ★ Don't miss aperitif time when customers spill out onto the pavement and take over the street.

Radetzky Café (13)
corso Garibaldi 105 ☎ 026572645

Ⓜ 2 Moscova 🕐 Tue.–Sun. 7–1am; closed Aug. ● prices vary

The Radetzky is a short distance from Brera. Journalists, writers and sophisticates frequently come here to enjoy breakfast, lunch, or Sunday brunch. There is a pleasant terrace in summer.

Not forgetting

■ **Bar Basso (14)** via Plinio 39 ☎ 0229400580 *19th-century decor and large rustic tables.*
■ **Café idriko (15)** via Celestino IV 11 *Under the beautiful apse of San Lorenzo: one of Milan's most trendy cafés.*
■ **Le Trottoir (16)** corso Garibaldi/via Tivoli ☎ 02801002 *Bar and restaurant until 11pm. Theme evenings, exhibitions, cultural events, jazz concerts.*
■ **Camparino (17)** galleria Vittorio Emanuele II ☎ 0286464435 *A Milan classic in the Galleria.*
■ **Stendhal Café (18)** via Ancona/via San Marco ☎ 026572059 *An elegant café.*

The bar is an integral part of Italian life: people go there in the morning for a capuccino, at midday for an espresso and in the evening for a martini with *tramezzini* (snacks) or pastries.

Basic facts

Heaving crowds, a range of music and the latest dance crazes are all standard in Milan's countless discos and nightclubs. It would be impossible to list them all, so we've just picked out the hottest spots. Some also organize concerts, themed evenings, shows and promotions.

 # After dark

Magazzini Generali (19)
via Pietrasanta 11 ☎ 0255211313

🚊 24, 90, 91 🕐 Wed.–Sun. 10pm–3am ● 15,000 lire–25,000 lire

This nightclub with its minimalist decor is housed in a former warehouse and has a large upstairs room and a disco on the first floor. ★ There is always something going on here: cultural events, photo exhibitions and concerts.

Shocking Club (20)
bastioni di Porta Nuova 12 ☎ 026595407

🚊 11, 29, 30, 33, 43 🕐 Tue.–Sat. 10.30pm–3am ● 20,000 lire–30,000 lire

The world of fashion's favorite club, frequented by top models, the Shocking Club does everything it can to live up to its name. Tuesday is students' night (revival/underground music); there's a theme night on Wednesday, guaranteed to be outrageous; and Thursday is given over to house music.

Hollywood (21)
corso Como 15 ☎ 026598996

Ⓜ 2 Garibaldi 🕐 Tue.–Sun. 10.30pm–4am ● 25,000 lire–30,000 lire

Lights and fluorescent colors, metal fittings and mirror globes decorate Milan's trendiest nightspot. Hollywood's customers include businessmen, models and celebrities who, not being able to leave their handprints in the dance floor, inscribe their names on the walls. ★ Note: rock night on Tuesday attracts a studenty crowd; Thursdays are theme nights and anniversary celebrations; Sundays the club is thronged with top models, showbiz and sports celebrities.

Propaganda (22)
via Castelbarco 11 ☎ 0258310682

🚊 9, 29, 30, 65, 79, 90, 91 🕐 Mon.–Tue., Thur.–Sun. 10pm–3am ● 13,000 lire–25,000 lire

This large disco, recently opened, is able to hold up to 2000 people. It is owned by the rock singer Vasco Rossi and showcases a wide range of bands. The atmosphere is metropolitan and high-tech, there are large screens, internet stations and a selection of foreign newspapers. There is a different sound each night of the week: Tuesday is live music (fusion and ambient); Friday is revival night with 1970s hits sometimes spun by Claudio Cecchetto, the famous Italian DJ who started this '70s night.

Not forgetting

■ **Gimmi's (23)** via Cellini 2 ☎ 0255188069 *'Historic' and ever popular. Bands until 1am, followed by a club until dawn.*
■ **Nepentha (24)** piazza Diaz 1 ☎ 02804837 *A traditional disco with Folon decor. The restaurant serves stylish meals in a cozy atmosphere. Chic customers.*

SHOCKING CLUB

The clubs reveal
Milan's trendy
side: at the
cutting edge
of fashion and
dance. Usually,
women gain
admittance more
easily than men.

Basic facts

The sound of jazz is heard in many different Milanese clubs but, on the *navigli* (canals) to the south, Capolinea (near the Naviglio Grande) and Scimmie (on Naviglio Pavese) are important centers for jazz lovers. Fans of cabaret and comedy shows should try Bolgia Umana,

After dark

Scimmie (25)
via Ascanio Sforza 49 ☎ 0289402874

🔲 *59, 90, 91* 🕐 *Mon., Wed.–Sun.; closed Aug.* **Live jazz** *10.30pm–1.30am* ● *entrance charge varies* 🍴 *8pm–2am* 🍸

A 60ft long barge, moored on Naviglio Pavese, is the venue for this tiny, smoky club. In the 1980s a number of jazz musicians, including some big names, started coming here to jam. You can also hear rock and blues. An adjoining restaurant serves meals till late. In the club you can buy cocktails, beer and cold snacks; on the deck, drinks and sandwiches are available.

Capolinea (26)
via Lodovico il Moro 119 ☎ 0289122024

🔲 *2* 🕐 *Tue.–Sun.; closed Aug.* **Live jazz** *10pm–1.30am* ● *15,000 lire* 🍴 *7.30pm–12.30am* 🍸

Capolinea gets its name from the nearby no. 19 tram terminus (*capolinea* in Italian). The club, located in south Milan, opposite the Naviglio Grande, has been a venue for some of the biggest names in jazz since the 1950s. You can hear all kinds of jazz performed here: dixieland, bebop, hard bop, New Orleans, free jazz and fusion. The restaurant serves good home-made cooking. There are spontaneous jam sessions.

Grilloparlante (27)
alzaia Naviglio Grande 36 ☎ 0289409321

🔲 *29, 30* 🕐 *daily 8pm–2am* 🕐 **Shows** *Wed.–Mon. 10.30pm–1am* 🍴 *daily 8pm–1am* 🍸

This memorable club at Naviglio Grande puts on amazing shows, featuring a variety of different types of bands. You'll even spot the occasional celebrity in the audience. There is also an elegant restaurant with works by contemporary artists on display. In good weather dinner and music take place in the huge garden.

Club 2 (28)
via Formentini 2 ☎ 0286464807

🔲 *3, 4, 12, 61* 🕐 *daily 8.30pm–3am* ● *15,000 lire* 🍸 🍽

This is a fashionable bar that tends to attract chic customers. You can chat here without having to shout yourself hoarse over loud music. The club also has a disco. A wide variety of different sounds is on offer, including Latin-American, funk, reggae and easy-listening. Smart dress is advised.

Not forgetting

■ **Ca' Bianca Club (29)** via Lodovico il Moro 117 ☎ 0289125777 *Music and cabaret, right next to Capolinea.*
■ **Blues Canal by Gattullo (30)** via Casale 7 ☎ 028360799 *Jazz, blues and funk in this new premises. Restaurant open late.*
■ **Tangram (31)** via Pezzotti 52 ☎ 0289501007 *Jazz club.*

and piano bar enthusiasts
should settle down in Club 2.

Capolinea is Milan's premier jazz club, opened
by drummer Giorgio Vanni in the 1960s.

Guided tours
Società Autostradale *piazza Castello 1*
☎ *02801161* organizes bus tours of
Milan, conducted in various languages.

What to see

Milan from above

The highest point in Milan is the tip of the Duomo ➡ 86 – almost
high. From the roof, on a clear day, you can see the Pre-alps and Alps in
the distance. Milan nestles in a dip at the foot of the Alps and as a result
experiences fairly cold winters and sultry summers.

48
Sights
THE INSIDER'S FAVORITES

A brief history of Milan

222 BC
Mediolanum
comes under
Roman rule.
5th century
Milan becomes
the capital of the
western Roman

Empire.
**8th–12th
centuries**
Successive
occupations.
1262–1447
The Visconti
family rule Milan

and build the
Duomo.
1448–1535
The Sforza rule.
18th century
Austrian
occupation.
1796 Napoleon

is king of Italy
and makes Milan
the capital of
his Cisalpine
Republic.
1860 Garibaldi's
ideas triumph
with unification.

the area

Piazza del Duomo is the true center of Milan. It contains some of the city's most important monuments: the Duomo, the Galleria and the Palazzo Reale. ■ Where to stay ➡ 18 ➡ 20 ■ Where to eat ➡ 44 ➡ 70 ■ After dark ➡ 78 ■ Where to shop ➡ 120 ➡ 144

➡ What to see

Duomo (1)
piazza del Duomo ☎ 0286463456

M / Duomo; 3 Duomo ⊙ open daily 6.45am–7pm **Roof** summer: 9am–5.45pm; winter: 9am–4.45pm; closed Christmas, May 1st, Apr. 25 ● 6000 lire (8000 lire with lift, left transept) ⬙

Milan has the third largest cathedral after St Peter's in Rome and the cathedral of Seville. Work began in 1386 and continued for several centuries. Its architecture is a mixture of styles: the apse is Gothic, the façade combines baroque, neoclassical and neo-Gothic. On the highest of the 135 spires stands the gilt statue of the Madonnina (12ft high), the symbol of Milan. The detail of the façade gives way to a sober interior: it is divided into five naves, separated by 52 columns and illuminated by stained-glass windows with ornate tracery. ★ The walk on the roof among a forest of flying buttresses, gargoyles and statues is breathtaking.

Museo del Duomo (2)
piazza del Duomo 14 ☎ 02860358

M / Duomo; 3 Duomo ⊙ Tue.–Sun. 9.30am–12.30pm, 3–6pm; closed Christmas, Easter, May 1, April 25 ● 10000 lire

The cathedral museum houses displays of sculpture, fragments of masonry, sketches, models and stained-glass windows all documenting the long history of the cathedral's construction.

Palazzo Reale (3)
piazza del Duomo 12

M / Duomo; 3 Duomo ⊙ opening times vary (depending on exhibitions) ● admission charge varies

The Royal Palace, just to the right of the Duomo, was rebuilt between 1772 and 1778 by the architect Giuseppe Piermarini on the site of a 14th-century Visconti family palace. It suffered severe bomb-damage in 1943; traces of the destruction are still visible in the sala dei Cariatidi.

Galleria Vittorio Emanuele II (4)

M / Duomo; 3 Duomo

The Galleria was designed by Giuseppe Mengoni in 1864 and links piazza del Duomo and piazza della Scala. Since then this magnificent glass-roofed arcade has housed some of Milan's most fashionable bars and restaurants, among them the Camparino bar ➡ 78 and Savini restaurant ➡ 44.

Not forgetting

■ **Cimac (Civico Museo di Arte Contemporanea) (5)** piazza del Duomo 12 ☎ 0262083219 ⊙ Tue.–Sun. 9.30am–5.30pm *Houses numerous 20th-century Italian masterpieces.*
■ **Pinacoteca Ambrosiana (6)** piazza Pio XI 2 ☎ 02806921 ⊙ Tue.–Sun. 10am–4.30pm *Italian (Caravaggio, Botticelli, Ghirlandaio, Bramantino), Flemish and German art collections.*

The Duomo symbolizes Milan's grandeur and the Galleria its effortless elegance.

In the area

La Scala is probably Milan's most famous building. In the middle of piazza della Scala stands a statue of Leonardo da Vinci. Opposite is Palazzo Marino, now the city's municipal offices. ■ Where to stay ➡ 18 ➡ 28 ■ Where to eat ➡ 44 ➡ 46 ■ After dark ➡ 74 ➡ 78 ■ Where to

What to see

Teatro alla Scala (7)
piazza della Scala 1 ☎ 0272003744

M 1 Duomo; 3 Duomo 🚇 access via the Museo Teatrale

La Scala ➡ 74, the world-famous opera house, was built by Giuseppe Piermarini on the site of the church of Santa Maria della Scala, and inaugurated in 1778. The splendid horseshoe shaped auditorium, upholstered in red and gold velvet, has four balconies (with 260 boxes), two galleries and an orchestra. La Scala is also renowned for its excellent acoustics. In 1999 the theater will be closed for renovation work and is due to reopen in 2001 in time for the centenary of Verdi's death.

Museo Teatrale alla Scala (8)
via Filodrammatici 2 ☎ 028053418 ➡ 0286463170

M 1 Duomo; 3 Duomo ⏰ May–Oct.: open daily 9am–noon, 2–5pm; Nov.–Apr. same opening times but closed on Sun. ● 6000 lire 🚇 visits by arrangement 🏢

Established in 1901, this museum traces the history of theater, opera and La Scala through its vast collection of masks, costumes, scenery, musical instruments and scores. ★ Two rooms contain Verdi memorabilia, including the spinet on which he learned to play at the age of eight.

Museo Poldi Pezzoli (9)
via Alessandro Manzoni 12 ☎ 02794889 ➡ 028690788

M 3 Montenapoleone ⏰ Oct.–Mar.: Tue.–Fri. 9.30am–12.30pm, 2.30–6pm; Sat.–Sun. 9.30am–12.30pm, 2.30–7.30pm; Apr.–Sep. same opening times but closed Sun. pm ● 10,000 lire; combined ticket for Museo Poldi Pezzoli/Bagatti Valsecchi 14,0000 lire 🚇 visits by arrangement 🏢

The house of the great art collector, Gian Giacomo Poldi Pezzoli, was opened to the public after his death in 1879. The Poldi Pezzoli foundation houses masterpieces from the 15th to 18th centuries, including Pollaiolo's famous *Portrait of a Young Woman* (c. 1450), two Botticellis and a Madonna by Mantegna. There is also an extraordinary array of clocks and sundials, and a major collection of decorative arts.

Palazzo Marino (10)
piazza della Scala ☎ 0272000705

M 1 Duomo; 3 Duomo 🚇 visits by arrangement

This is one of the city's most beautiful *palazzi*. It was built in 1557 for the Genoese banker, Tommaso Marino, Duke of Terranova. It now houses the city's municipal offices. Marianna de Leyva, Marino's niece was born here. She was the inspiration for the nun of Monza, one of the characters in Alessandro Manzoni's famous novel, *I Promessi Sposi* (1827).

Not forgetting

■ **Museo Bagatti Valsecchi (11)** via Santo Spirito 10 ☎ 0276006132 ➡ 02760 14859 ⏰ Tue.–Sun. 1–5pm *Collection of Renaissance art.*
■ **Museo di Milano (12)** via Sant'Andrea 6 ☎ 02783 797 ⏰ Tue.–Sun. 9am–6pm *Prints, furniture and artifacts tracing the history of Milan.*

shop ➡ 120
➡ 124 ➡ 126
➡ 128 ➡ 130
➡ 132

Montenapoleone **M**

Via Brera
Via Monte di Pietà
Via Andegari
Via Verdi
Via Alessandro Manzoni
Via Bigli
Via Monte Napoleone
Via S. Spirito
Via Gesù
Via S. Andrea
Via Bagutta
Via Verri
PALAZZO BELGIOIOSO
Piazza della Scala
Piazza Meda
Corso Matteotti
Piazza S. Babila
S. Babila **M**

La Scala è ricostruita. Dirige Toscanini.

Fiducia in Dio was the favorite sculpture of Gian Giacomo Poldi Pezzoli's mother.

CARUSO

In the area

In the 18th century, corso Venezia rivaled corso di Porta Romana in elegance and was at the center of Milanese intellectual life. Visitors can still admire the majestic buildings lining the corso, particularly Palazzo Serbelloni and Palazzo Castiglione. ■ Where to stay ➡ 28 ➡ 30 ■ Where to eat

What to see

Giardini pubblici (13)
Entrances in porta Venezia, via Palestro, via Manin

Ⓜ / Palestro Ⓞ *summer 6am–11pm; winter 7.30am–5pm*

Between 1783 and 1786, Giuseppe Piermarini, architect of La Scala ➡ 88, came up with the idea of joining the gardens belonging to the convents on corso Venezia into one large park. It was further enlarged in 1862 when Giuseppe Balzaretto added the grounds belonging to the adjacent Dugnani Palazzo. ★ The park is a good place to take children: there are pony rides, a zoo, merry-go-rounds, and kiosks selling refreshments.

Museo Civico di Storia Naturale (14)
corso Venezia 55 ☎ 02781312 ➡ 0276022287

Ⓜ / Palestro Ⓞ *Mon.–Fri 9am–6pm; Sat.–Sun. 9.30am–6.30pm* ● *admission free* 🗓 *Mon.–Fri 9am–noon* ☎ *02783528* 🈺

The museum was opened in 1893. Visitors with a fascination for natural history can find interesting collections of rocks and minerals, dinosaur and other fossils, zoological specimens including a remarkable display of insects, and a well-presented botanical section. There is also a specialist bookstore and library.

Planetario Ulrico Hoepli (15)
corso Venezia 57 ☎ 0229531181

Ⓜ / Palestro Ⓞ **Shows** *Tue., Thur. 9pm, Sat., Sun. 3pm and 4.30pm* ● *4000 lire*

The Planetarium, designed by Portaluppi, was bequeathed to the city in 1930 by the publisher Hoepli. Visitors are invited to observe the stars and planets and follow their trajectories.

Villa Reale (16)
via Palestro 16 ☎ 0276002819

Ⓜ / Palestro; 3 Turati **Gardens** Ⓞ *summer–fall 9am–7pm; winter 9am–4pm; spring 9am–6pm*

Leopoldo Pollack built this neoclassical villa between 1790 and 1793 for count Barbiano di Belgiojoso. Among the illustrious guests who stayed here were Napoleon and Josephine, Count Radetzky and Napoleon III. Pollack also laid out the romantic Giardini di Villa Reale (gardens) with their mock Roman ruins. The villa now houses a gallery of modern art (Galleria d'Arte Moderna).

Not forgetting

■ **PAC (Padiglione d'Arte Contemporanea) (17)** via Palestro 14 ☎ 02783 330 Ⓞ Tue.–Sun. 9.30am–6.30pm *Rebuilt according to the original architectural designs drawn up by Gardella in 1953.*
■ **Galleria d'Arte Moderna (18)** via Palestro 16 ☎ 02760 02819 Ⓞ Tue.–Sun. 9.30am–5.30pm *A large collection of 19th- and early 20th-century Italian art, including* The Fourth Estate *(1901), Giuseppe Pellizza da Volpedo's painting symbolizing the emergence of the working class.*

➡ 46 ➡ 52
◼ Where
to shop
➡ 132

14

13

15

18

14

16

In the area

The Porta Romana district gets its name from the Roman road that used to run through it. Near the Università degli Studi runs corso Porta Romana, which, until the end of the 18th century, was Milan's most elegant street and a magnet for the city's nobility. ■ Where to stay ➤ 20 ■ Where

What to see

Ca' Granda (19)
via Festa del Perdono 7 ☎ 0258351

M *1 Duomo; 3 Duomo, Missori* 🕐 *Mon.–Fri. 9am–noon* ● *admission free*

The beautiful Ca'Granda, now the University Department of Humanities and Law, was originally built as a hospital, the Spedal Grande de la Nunciata, during the Renaissance. Its construction started in 1456 under the Duke of Milan, Francesco Sforza, but it wasn't until the 17th century that work was finally completed. In 1939, the hospital's functions were transferred to Niguarda and the Ca'Granda was taken over by the university. It was destroyed by bombs in 1939, but was completely rebuilt in the 1950s and has recently been restored further.

San Nazaro Maggiore (20)
corso di Porta Romana ☎ 0258307719

M *1 Duomo; 3 Duomo, Missori* 🕐 *7am–noon, 2.30–7pm* ● *admission free (donations welcome)* 🔲 *visits by arrangement with the priest*

Bishop Ambrose of Milan commissioned the construction of the original church in 386. Close to the entrance is the Capella Trivulzio, built in 1512 by Bramantino. This was designed to house the tomb of Marshal Gian Giacomo Trivulzio, who ruled Milan on behalf of the French at the beginning of the 16th century. Inside the church there are some remarkable frescos by Daniele Crespi (16th–17th century) and in the Capella Santa Caterina, on the left side of the transept, can be seen Bernadino Lanino's 16th-century masterpiece, *The Martyrdom of St Catherine.*

Torre Velasca (21)
piazza Velasca

M *3 Missori*

The Torre Velasca was built in 1958 by BBPR, one of Milan's leading firms of architects where Peressutti, Rogers and Belgiojoso worked. One unusually distinctive feature can be seen at the top of the 26-story reinforced concrete tower, where the highest 6 floors are corbeled in the style of a medieval tower.

Santa Maria presso San Satiro (22)
via Speronari 3 ☎ 02874683

M *3 Duomo, Missori* 🕐 *open daily 8.30–11.30am, 3.30–5.30 pm* ● *admission free (donations welcome)*

★ This small church is dedicated to Satiro Donato, the brother of Saint Ambrose. It contains an extraordinary *trompe l'oeil* by Donato Bramante. Through a skillful combination of frescos and niches he managed to create the illusion of an apse extending beyond the high altar. The beautiful octagonal baptistry off the right aisle was also designed by Bramante and contains terracottas by Agosto de Fondutis.

to eat ➡ 64
■ After
dark ➡ 76
➡ 80

19

19

22

22

20

21

22

In the area

The Ticinese district, which owes its name to the River Ticino, is a traditionally working-class area. Many of its stores and tenement blocks are now being renovated. ■ Where to eat ➡ 62 ➡ 68 ➡ 70 ■ Where to shop ➡ 142 ➡ 144

What to see

San Lorenzo Maggiore (23)
corso di Porta Ticinese ☎ 0289404129

🔲 3, 94 🕐 open daily 9.30am–6.30pm ● 2000 lire

The basilica, founded in the 4th century, has undergone extensive alteration, though its original octagonal design has been preserved. ★ The beautiful 4th-century Capella Sant'Aquilino is the highlight of the church and contains a splendid mosaic representing Christ with His apostles.

Colonne di San Lorenzo (24)
corso di Porta Ticinese

🔲 3, 94

Opposite the basilica stands a row of 16 Roman Corinthian columns. They are the ruins of an Ancient Roman temple and were transferred here in the 4th century to form a portico, which is no longer standing. Beside the columns is a copy of a Roman statue of the Emperor Constantine.

Parco delle Basiliche (25)
piazza della Vetra

🔲 3, 94 🕐 free admission, open daily

Piazza della Vetra is just behind the church of San Lorenzo. In ancient times it was the place where numerous water courses converged before flowing into the network of canals (navigli). This was the spot where the scaffold stood for seven centuries until 1840. Now this large green expanse forms the Parco delle Basiliche.

Sant'Eustorgio (26)
piazza Sant'Eustorgio 1 ☎ 0258101583

🔲 3, 15 🕐 open daily 7.30am–noon, 3–7pm ● admission free (donations welcome)

The foundations of the basilica go back to the 7th century. It was rebuilt in 1278 and a campanile was added in 1309. The side chapels were built in the 15th century and decorated with early Renaissance art. The façade was rebuilt in 1862–65. One of the chapels is dedicated to the Magi; their supposed relics were brought to Milan by Saint Eustorgio and carried off to Cologne by the Emperor Frederic Barbarossa in 1164. Behind the crypt is the Portinari chapel attributed to Michelozzo and decorated with frescos by Vincenzo Foppa. The chapel finally reopened in October 1998 after extensive restoration work.

Not forgetting

■ **Porta Ticinese medievale (27)** corso di Porta Ticinese Built in the 14th century and restored in 1861.
■ **Porta Ticinese (28)** piazza XXIV Maggio Built in 1804 by Luigi Cagnola to celebrate the Battle of Marengo.
■ **Darsena (29)** piazza XXIV Maggio/viale D'Annunzio Milan's old docks

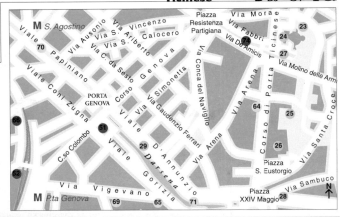

23

23

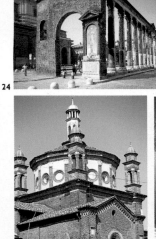

24

The lively Ticinese district, an area rich in history, bears many traces of its Ancient Roman past.

26

26

26

In the area

The beautiful basilica is at the heart of the Sant'Ambrogio district. Elegant town houses and lovely *palazzi* fringe the piazza, and just behind the basilica is the Università Cattolica. ■ Where to stay ➡ 26 ■ After dark ➡ 74 ➡ 78 ■ Where to shop ➡ 140

What to see

Sant'Ambrogio (30)
piazza Sant'Ambrogio 25 ☎ 028057310

Ⓜ 2 Sant'Ambrogio 🕙 *open daily 9.30am–noon, 2.30–6pm* ● *admission free (donations welcome)*

Milan's most important basilica was founded in 379 by the city's patron saint, Saint Ambrose and is his last resting place. Sant'Ambrogio is one of the finest examples of medieval sacred architecture. The pulpit, carved in 1080 and set on a late Roman sarcophagus, is a medieval masterpiece ★. Two other treasures grace the sanctuary: the 9th-century ciborium, supported by four porphyry columns, and the high altar (835), encrusted with enamel, gold, silver and precious stones and attributed to Volvinio.

Museo della Scienza e della Tecnica Leonardo da Vinci (31)
via San Vittore 21 ☎ 02485551 ➡ 0248010016

Ⓜ 2 Sant'Ambrogio 🕙 *Tue.–Fri. 9.30am–4.50pm; Sat., Sun. and public holidays 9.30am–6.20pm* ● *10,000 lire; under-18s and over-60s 6000 lire* 🔲 🔳 ⊞ ♿

This science and technology museum, housed in a former monastery (San Vittore), is divided into 28 sections. The Leonardo da Vinci gallery ★ displays wooden models and explanations of his machines and inventions.

Santa Maria delle Grazie (32)
via G.A. Sassi 3 ☎ 0248021416

Ⓜ 1 Cadorna, Conciliazione 🕙 *open daily 8am–noon, 3–7pm* ● *admission free (donations welcome)*

Built in the 15th century by Guiniforte Solari, this church was later modified by Bramante. He added the tribune with its 16-sided dome in 1492 and also designed the cloister and the sacristy, restored in 1982.

Cenacolo Vinciano (33)
piazza Santa Maria delle Grazie 2 ☎ 024987588

Ⓜ 1 Cadorna, Conciliazione 🕙 *Tue.–Sat. 8am–1.45pm, 7–9.45pm; Sun. 8am–1.45pm, 5–8pm* ● *12,000 lire* 🔲

Leonardo da Vinci painted his *Last Supper* on the refectory wall of the convent of Santa Maria delle Grazie. His technique of painting on glue and plaster, and the humidity, has made conservation difficult.

Not forgetting

■ **Pusterla di Sant'Ambrogio (34)** via De Amicis/via San Vittore ☎ 028053505 🕙 *open daily 10am–7pm This 12th-century gate now houses the Museo della Criminolgia e Armi Antichi (museum of crime and antique weapons).*
■ **Palazzo Litta (35)** corso Magenta 24 *A huge rococo palace (1763), begun in 1648 by Carla Maria Richini. It houses the Teatro Litta.*
■ **Civico Museo Archeologico (36)** corso Magenta 15 ☎ 02864 50011 🕙 *Tue.–Sun. 9.30am–5.50pm Roman, Etruscan and Greek artifacts.*

33
Working in
Milan under
Ludovico il
Moro, da Vinci
produced a
number of
works of art.

In the area

Piazza d'Armi in front of Castello Sforzesco used to be a parade ground and marks the limits of the old city walls. Napoleon wanted to build a Roman-style forum here to be known as the Foro Bonaparte, but all that remains of this project is a semicircular road south of the castle.

→ What to see

Castello Sforzesco (37)
piazza Castello ☎ 0262083191

Ⓜ *I Cairoli; 2 Lanza* 🕙 *7am–6pm* ● *admission free*

The Castello is often described as Milan's most important Renaissance building, although its present appearance owes much to rebuilding at the turn of the century. However, some of the original features remain. Originally a fortress (1368), it was razed to the ground by the Ambrosian Republic in 1447 and rebuilt three years later under Franceso Sforza. The beautiful courtyard, Cortile della Rocchetta, survives from this period. Corte Ducale (1473) also remains. The tower at the main entrance is a reconstruction of the original built by Filarete in 1452 and destroyed by lightning a century later.

Musei del Castello (38)
piazza Castello ☎ 0262083940

Ⓜ *I Cairoli; 2 Lanza* 🕙 *Tue.–Sun. 9am–5.30pm* ● *free*

The Castello houses a number of museums, most of them located in Corte Ducale. ★ The sculpture collection includes one of Michelangelo's last works, the unfinished *Pietà Rondanini*. The Pinacoteca contains works by Mantegna (*Virgin and Saints*), Giovanni Bellini (*Madonna and Child*), Tintoretto (*The prosecutor Soranzo's family*), and Vincenzo Foppa (*Saint Sebastian*) among others. It also has a collection of decorative art (ceramics, gold and silver plate, ivory, enamel work, bronzes.) The museum of musical instruments holds 640 string and wind instruments. The Achille Bertarelli collection comprises almost a million different pieces, including portraits, stamps, publicity posters and photographs.

38

37

38

The sculpted head of Theodolinda, the Lombard queen, who converted to orthodox Christianity.

38

■ Where to stay ➡ 26
■ Where to eat ➡ 48
■ After dark ➡ 78 ➡ 82
■ Where to shop ➡ 134

Parco Sempione (39)
Entrances in piazza Castello, viale Alemagna, piazza Sempione, via Legnano

Ⓜ *I Cairoli, Cadorna; 2 Lanza, Cadorna* ☉ *summer 6am–11pm; winter 7.30am–5pm, Dec. 7.30am–4.30pm*

The park, laid out on the former parade ground of the Castello Sforzesco, was designed by Emilio Alemagna in 1893. Within it is Palazzo dell'Arte, the work of Giovanni Muzio (1933), where the Milan Triennial of modern architecture and design is held.

Not forgetting

■ **Arco della Pace (40)** piazza Sempione *Commissioned by Napoleon to glorify his conquests but in 1838 it was dedicated to peace by the Habsburgs.* ■ **Acquario (41)** viale Gadio 2 ☎ 0286462051 ☉ Tue.–Sun. 9.30am–5.30pm *An aquarium with a huge variety of fish.* ■ **Santa Maria del Carmine (42)** piazza del Carmine 2 ☎ 02864 63365 ☉ *open daily 7.30–11.30am; 3–7pm 15th-century church with 19th-century façade by Carlo Maciachini.* ■ **Fondazione Antonio Mazzotta (43)** Foro Buonaparte 50 ☎ 02878197 ☉ Wed., Fri.–Sun. 10am–7.30pm; Tue., Thur. 10am–10.30pm *This museum houses a permanent collection and exhibits work by internationally famous artists.*

39

38

In the area

Brera once had a reputation as an artists' quarter and until recently it was home to numerous artisans' workshops. Nowadays you are more likely to find antique stores, late-night bars and art galleries. ■ Where to eat ➡ 48 ➡ 50 ■ After dark ➡ 78 ■ Where to shop ➡ 134

What to see

Palazzo di Brera (44)
via Brera 28

Ⓜ *1 Cairoli; 2 Lanza; 3 Montenapoleone* **Observatory** ☎ 02723201 Ⓢ *Mon.–Fri. 8.30am–noon, 12.30–4.30pm* **Braidense Library** ☎ 0286463484 Ⓢ *Mon.–Fri 9am–5pm; Sat. 9am–1.30pm* ● *free*

In 1572, members of the Jesuit order decided to settle here on a *brayda* (the local word for a piece of uncultivated land, from which the name Brera comes), and construct a palace. The two most striking features of the building are the colonnaded central court, built in 1651 and the gate added by Giuseppe Piermarini in 1774. During the Austrian occupation of the city, when they temporarily suppressed religious orders, the palace was transformed into a cultural center, comprising the Observatory, the Brera library, the botanical garden (which is not open to the public) and the Academy of Fine Arts, the first of its kind in Milan. Napoleon, whose bronze statue (by Antonio Canova, 1811) is in the center of the courtyard, made a significant contribution to the academy's collection of art treasures. Many rooms had to be rebuilt after bombs damaged the building in 1943.

Pinacoteca di Brera (45)
via Brera 28 ☎ 02722631

Ⓜ *1 Cairoli; 2 Lanza; 3 Montenapoleone* Ⓢ *Tue.–Sat. 9am–10pm; Sun. 9am–1.30pm, 2.30–8pm* ● *8000 lire; under-18s and over-60s free* 🎫 🖥 ⊞

The Pinacoteca (Academy of Fine Arts), housed in the Palazzo di Brera, has been open to public view since 1809. It contains some of Italy's greatest art treasures from the 15th century to the present day.
★ Among the most outstanding are Mantegna's *The Dead Christ*, Raphael's *Marriage of the Virgin*, Giovanni Bellini's *Virgin and Child* and also his *Pietà*. There are also some remarkable frescos from the Mocchirolo oratory, which are attributed to artists from the school of Giovanni da Milano, as well as many paintings by other European masters such as Rembrandt, Van Dyck and El Greco. The Jesi collection boasts a fine collection of 20th-century art and prides itself on its particular focus on Italian art from 1910 to 1930.

Not forgetting

■ **Museo del Risorgimento (46)** via Borgonuovo 23 ☎ 028693549 Ⓢ *Tue.–Sun. 9.30am–5.30pm Paintings and artifacts dating from the Italian Risorgimento (the uprising of Italy against the Austrians resulting in unification), housed in Palazzo Morigia.*
■ **San Marco (47)** piazza San Marco 2 ☎ 0229002598 Ⓢ *open daily 7.30am–noon, 4–7pm Milan's second largest church after the Duomo. It has undergone several rebuildings since its dedication in 1254 (only the original portal still survives). It contains some fine paintings.*
■ **San Simpliciano (48)** piazza San Simpliciano 7 ☎ 02862274 Ⓢ *open daily 7.10am–noon, 3–7pm; public holidays 7.30am–12.30pm, 4–7pm Founded by Bishop Ambrose in the 4th century. The church underwent substantial restoration work in the 11th and 12th centuries. Adjoining it are two splendid 15th- and 16th-century cloisters.*

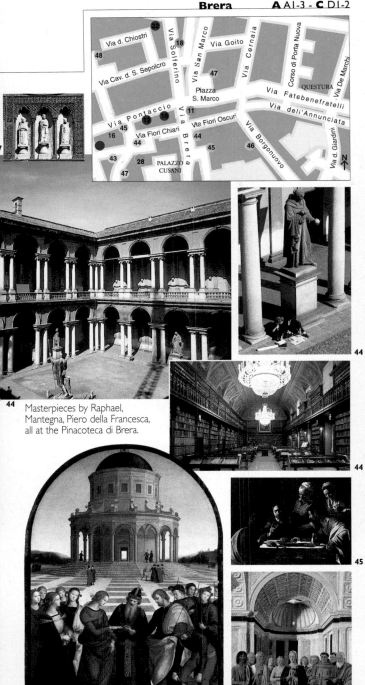

Masterpieces by Raphael,
Mantegna, Piero della Francesca,
all at the Pinacoteca di Brera.

Cycling in the countryside
The ban on cars in Parco del Ticino ➡ 116
makes it an ideal place for cyclists.
Information on cycle routes and bicycle hire:
☎ 0290849926

Further afield

Bergamo

Explore the underground remains of the walls built around Bergamo Alta ➡ 112 by the Venetians in the 16th century. Guided tours, for groups of 15 minimum, are organized by by the caving club *Le Nottole* ☎ *035251233* or ☎ *035241020*

Days out

THE INSIDER'S FAVORITES

Lake Como

Less than an hour away by train, Como is Milan's favorite weekend retreat. Some Milanese come here just to dine or even for a mid-week break. Trains leave from:
Stazione Ferrovie Nord Milano piazzale Cadorna ☎ *0248066771*
Boat trips on Lake Como are run by:
Navigazione Lariana ☎ *031304060*

INDEX BY TYPE

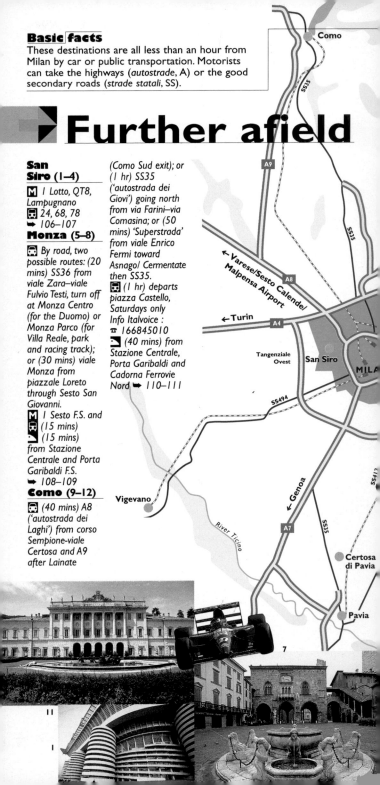

Basic facts

These destinations are all less than an hour from Milan by car or public transportation. Motorists can take the highways (*autostrade*, A) or the good secondary roads (*strade statali*, SS).

▶ Further afield

San Siro (1–4)

M *1 Lotto, QT8, Lampugnano*

24, 68, 78

➡ *106–107*

Monza (5–8)

🚗 *By road, two possible routes: (20 mins) SS36 from viale Zara–viale Fulvio Testi, turn off at Monza Centro (for the Duomo) or Monza Parco (for Villa Reale, park and racing track); or (30 mins) viale Monza from piazzale Loreto through Sesto San Giovanni.*

M *1 Sesto F.S. and (15 mins) (15 mins) from Stazione Centrale and Porta Garibaldi F.S.*

➡ *108–109*

Como (9–12)

🚗 *(40 mins) A8 ('autostrada dei Laghi') from corso Sempione–viale Certosa and A9 after Lainate*

(Como Sud exit); or (1 hr) SS35 ('autostrada dei Giovi') going north from via Farini–via Comasina; or (50 mins) 'Superstrada' from viale Enrico Fermi toward Asnago/ Cermenate then SS35.

🚌 *(1 hr) departs piazza Castello, Saturdays only Info Italvoice :* ☎ *166845010*

🚆 *(40 mins) from Stazione Centrale, Porta Garibaldi and Cadorna Ferrovie Nord* ➡ *110–111*

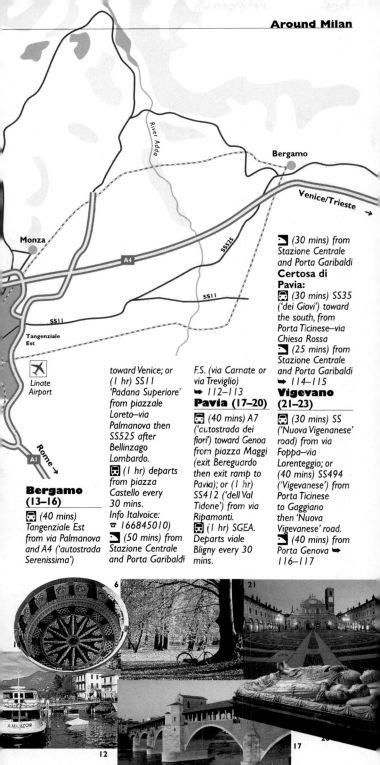

🚆 (30 mins) from Stazione Centrale and Porta Garibaldi

Certosa di Pavia:

🚌 (30 mins) SS35 ('dei Giovi') toward the south, from Porta Ticinese–via Chiesa Rossa

🚆 (25 mins) from Stazione Centrale and Porta Garibaldi ➡ 114–115

Vigevano (21–23)

🚌 (30 mins) SS ('Nuova Vigenanese' road) from via Foppa–via Lorenteggio; or (40 mins) SS494 ('Vigevanese') from Porta Ticinese to Gaggiano then 'Nuova Vigevanese' road.

🚆 (40 mins) from Porta Genova ➡ 116–117

✈ Linate Airport

toward Venice; or (1 hr) SS11 'Padana Superiore' from piazzale Loreto–via Palmanova then SS525 after Bellinzago Lombardo.

🚌 (1 hr) departs from piazza Castello every 30 mins.
Info Italvoice: ☎ 166845010)

🚆 (50 mins) from Stazione Centrale and Porta Garibaldi

Bergamo (13–16)

🚌 (40 mins) Tangenziale Est from via Palmanova and A4 ('autostrada Serenissima')

F.S. (via Carnate or via Treviglio) ➡ 112–113

Pavia (17–20)

🚌 (40 mins) A7 ('autostrada dei fiori') toward Genoa from piazza Maggi (exit Bereguardo then exit ramp to Pavia); or (1 hr) SS412 ('dell Val Tidone') from via Ripamonti.

🚌 (1 hr) SGEA. Departs viale Bligny every 30 mins.

Basic facts

The San Siro neighborhood, northwest of the city, near the Fiera, owes its name to a little 15th-century church: San Siro alla Vepra. The area is home to the Giuseppe Meazza stadium and the racecourse.

Further afield

Stadio Civico Giuseppe Meazza (1)
via dei Piccolomini 5 ☎ 0248700457

🚌 24 🅿 ℹ Info ☎ 0248700457 🕐 Mon.–Sat. 9am–noon ● 12,000 lire

The stadium, built in 1926 and originally called San Siro, was modernized in 1955 by the architects Calzolario and Ronca and can now hold 80,000 spectators. In 1980, it was dedicated to Giuseppe 'Peppino' Meazza, Italy's famous captain of the national soccer team from 1934 to 1938. The roof, which was constructed in 1990 for the soccer World Cup, is built on eight columns, all placed outside the stadium so as to preserve the 1950s structure.

Ippodromo di San Siro (2)
piazzale dello Sport ☎ 02482161

Ⓜ 1 Lotto 🚌 78 🅿 🕐 Mar.–Nov.: open daily 2.45–6.30pm ● 8000 lire–10,000 lire

This racecourse, inaugurated in 1921, holds races on the flat and over jumps. ★ Adjoining the racecourse is a botanical garden containing some very rare plants.

Trotter (3)
via dei Piccolomini 2 ☎ 02482161

🚌 78 🅿 🕐 daytime races 2.45–6.30pm; eve. races (mid-May–Sep.) 8.30–11.30pm ● 8000 lire–10,000 lire

Built in 1925 to host trotting races, the Trotter was completely renovated after World War II. A closed-circuit system, with screens positioned at various points, enables spectators to follow every stage of the race.

Monte Stella (4)
via Terzaghi

Ⓜ 1 QT8, Lampugnano 🚌 68 🅿 🌿

This 'mountain' has a tragic history. It was built using the rubble that resulted from wartime bombing and then it was enlarged with stones from the fortifications around the city that were demolished in the post war years. In the 1960s, the earth that was removed in the course of digging the foundations for new apartment blocks was also added. Today the terraced 'mountain' stands at a height of around 500ft. It has been landscaped and now attracts lots of weekend visitors. ★ From the top there is a good view of the stadium and racecourse, and on a clear day you can even see as far as the foothills of the Alps.

Not forgetting

■ **Ribot** via Cremosano 41 ☎ 0233001646 🕐 Tue.–Sun.; closed Christmas, New Year, Aug. *This restaurant, just behind the racecourse, is frequented by the horse-racing crowd. It serves classic cuisine and there is a lovely terrace to sit out on in warmer weather.*

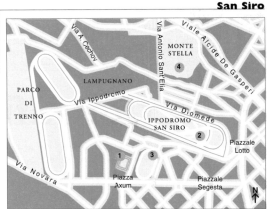

The Meazza stadium as it was (above) and as it is now (left) with its futurist architecture.

Basic facts

Monza is about nine miles north of Milan. It dates back to pre-Roman times, but its golden age was under the Lombards. It fell to the Visconti in 1324 and later to the Spanish, and finally to the Austrians. Monza underwent a period of rapid economic development in the 19th century

Further afield

Villa Reale (5)
viale Regina Margherita 2

⊡ visits by appointment ☎ 039323222 ◷ Tue.–Sun. from May–Oct. ● 5000 lire

The Villa Reale, built for the Archduke Ferdinand of Austria by Giuseppe Piermarini in the 18th century, is a masterpiece of neo-classical architecture.

Parco della Villa Reale/Parco di Monza (6)
☎ 039322003 or 384113

◷ Summer 7am–8.30pm, winter 7am–7pm ● free 🍴 🍸

This beautiful park, covering more than 1,970 acres, once belonged to the Villa Reale and was laid out in 1805 by Napoleonic decree. It is now home to several farms, a restaurant, an agricultural college, golf clubs, a racecourse, and Monza's famous motor-racing track.

Autodromo (7)
☎ 03924821

◷ 9am–6pm ● 10,000 lire (Formula One races) 🍴 🏟

This internationally renowned *autodromo* (motor-racing track), built in 1922, hosts the annual Italian Formula One races. The track is open to visitors by appointment. To book, telephone the secretary's office. While at the circuit, you can visit the racing drivers' restaurant, a specialist store and a bookstore.

Duomo (8)
piazza del Duomo ☎ 039323404

◷ Open daily 7.30–noon, 3–6.30pm ● admission free (donations welcome)
Crown and Treasury 9–11.30am, 3–5.30pm; opening times vary on public holidays ● 5000 lire (Crown and Treasury), 1500 lire (Crown), 4000 lire (Treasury)

The Duomo, or Basilica San Giovanni Battista, to give it its full name, was built in the 13th century on the site of a 6th-century church. It has a lovely green and white striped marble façade designed by Matteo da Campione (1396). ★ The chapel of the Lombard queen Theodolinda (left of the choir), contains the Iron Crown of Italy, in which one of the nails from the Cross of Christ is said to be embedded. The treasury houses numerous precious objects, including the 5th-century ivory diptych of Stilicho, a breviary belonging to Saint Charles Borromeo, censers, silver and gold plate.

Not forgetting

■ **Saint Georges Premier** in the park ☎ 039320600 ◷ Mon., Wed.–Sun.; closed week of Aug. 15 *A restaurant in an 18th-century hunting lodge, with period furniture, serving first-class cuisine.*
■ **Alle Grazie** via Lecco 84 ☎ 039387903 ◷ Mon.–Tue., Thur.–Sun.; closed Aug. *A restaurant occupying an old villa on the edge of the park. Tables outside on the terrace in warm weather.*

and is now one of Lombardy's economic powerhouses.

5

6

6

7

The treasures preserved in Monza's cathedral are kept in a splendid 3rd-century casket.

8

8

8

8

Basic facts

An hour's drive from Milan is Lake Como. Bordered with woods, little ports and luxury villas, it is about 30 miles long and forks into two in the middle. At the extreme southwest lies Como, an old Roman town, which from c.1050 to 1335 was an independent city state.

▶ Further afield

Duomo (9)
via Plinio ☎ 031300610

◐ *Open daily 7am–noon, 3–7pm* ● *free (donations welcome)*

Como's magnificent Duomo was built on the site of the Roman church of Santa Maria Maggiore. Work began in 1396 under architect Lorenzo degli Spazzi and was completed in 1740 with the construction of the dome by the late baroque master Filippo Juvarra. The façade, a harmonious blend of late Gothic and Renaissance styles, is decorated with numerous statues. The interior, in the shape of a Latin cross, is divided into three naves hung with nine splendid 16th-century tapestries. Fine paintings by Bernardino Luini and Gaudenzio Ferrari.

Broletto/Torre del Comune (10)
via Plinio

◐ *open only for exhibitions*

To the left of the Duomo is the town hall, or Broletto, with its red and white marble façade. Built in the 12th century, it was remodeled in the mid-15th century. Next to it is the Torre del Commune, built in the 13th century and completely reconstructed in 1927.

10

9

Villa Olmo (11)
via Cantoni ☎ 031252443

🕐 *open daily 8am–6pm; on public holidays apply to the doorkeeper:* ☎ 031574240
visits of the greenhouses ☎ 031571835 ● *free* 🏛

Villa Olmo is one of Como's most splendid villas. Its rooms contain
magnificent frescos and it has extensive grounds with views right across
the lake.

Lake Como (12)

A visit to Como wouldn't be complete without a boat trip. Departures
are every 30 minutes from the landing stage opposite piazza Cavour.
★ Cernobbio and Tremezzo (on the left bank) and Bellagio (on the right
bank) are among the prettiest towns on the lake. The shores also offer
plenty of quiet retreats.

Not forgetting

🔳 **Imbarcadero** piazza Cavour 20 ☎ 031270166 🕐 closed Dec. 26–
Jan. 6 *A restaurant housed in a 19th-century palazzo opposite the lake. The menu
varies with the seasons.*
🔳 **Crotto del Lupo** via Pisani Dossi 17 ☎ 031570 881 🕐 Tue.–Sun.;
closed Aug. *Good Lombard cuisine in a hillside setting.*

The Lake Como boat
is called a 'lucia', named
after the character in
Manzoni's novel.

Basic facts
Bergamo, on the edge of the Lombard plain, was founded by mountain Celts and subsequently taken over by the Romans, Venetians and finally Austrians in the 19th century. The upper town, Bergamo Alta, is medieval, and the lower town, Bergamo Bassa, is modern.

Further afield

Pinacoteca dell'Accademia Carrara (13)
via San Tommaso 53 ☎ 035399643 (town hall)

🕐 Wed.–Mon., Fri. 9.30am–12.30pm, 2.30–5.30pm ● 5000 lire; Sun. free
Gallery of modern art ☎ 035399 527 ● *opening times vary depending on exhibitions*

The neoclassical palace of the Accademia Carrara in the lower town houses one of the country's finest art collections. Its 15 rooms display works by all the major Italian artists: Sandro Botticelli, Vincenzo Foppa, Lorenzo Lotto, Giovanni Bellini and Andrea Mantegna. The gallery of modern art opposite was inaugurated in 1991 and houses a permanent collection of works by Manzu, Sironi, Campigli, Tosi, and Morlotti among others and also hosts temporary exhibitions.

Piazza Vecchia (14)
The *città alta* (upper town) can be reached by funicular or by car along viale Vittorio Emanuele 11. 15th-century piazza Vecchia is bordered by Palazzo Nuovo, which now houses a library, Palazzo del Podestà Veneto, the main university building, and Palazzo della Ragione, built at the end of the 12th century and restored by the Bergamasque architect Pietro Isabello.

Cappella Colleoni (15)
piazza del Duomo

🕐 *Mar.–Oct. open daily 9am–noon, 2–6.30pm; Nov.–Feb.: Tue.–Sun. 9am–noon, 2–5.30pm ● admission free*

Go through the gallery at the side of Palazzo della Ragione and you'll find the Colleoni chapel, a beautiful example of Lombard Renaissance art. It was built by Giovanni Antonio Amadeo between 1472 and 1476 for the Bergamasque condottiere Bartelomeo Colleoni.

Santa Maria Maggiore (16)
piazza del Duomo ☎ 035223327

🕐 *open daily 8am–noon, 3–6pm; public holidays 8–10.30am, 3–6pm ● admission free (donations welcome)*

The town erected this church to the Virgin to seek her help and protection when plague was sweeping through the population. It dates from 1137 and, despite later additions, is one of the finest Romanesque churches in Lombardy. It is decorated with 14th-century frescos. Splendid stalls by Lotto, Zenale and Previtali and Flemish and Tuscan tapestries. Composer Gaetano Donizetti is buried here.

Not forgetting
■ **Taverna del Colleoni–dell'Angelo** piazza Vecchia 7 ☎ 035232596
🕐 *Tue.–Sun. Excellent Lombard cuisine from chef Angelo Cornaro in a picturesque setting in the città alta.*
■ **Öl Giopì e la Margì** via Borgo Palazzo 27 ☎ (035) 242 366
🕐 *Tue.–Sun. noon; closed Jan., Aug. Authentic Bergamasque cuisine. Waiters, in traditional costume, speak local dialect.*

PORTA
S. ALESSANDRO
Piazza
Mascheroni
Via della Fara
Morla
BERGAMO ALTA
ROCCA
EX CONVENTO
DI S. AGOSTINO
14
Viale delle Mura
Piazza
Mercato
delle Scarpe
Via Porta Dipinta
PORTA
S. AGOSTINO
13
Piazza
G. Carrara
15
16
Viale delle Mura
Via San Tomaso
N
PORTA
S. GIACOMO
Viale Vittorio Emanuele II
PARCO
SUARDI

13

The *Mystical Wedding of St Catherine* (Lorenzo Lotto, 1480–1556) in the Accademia Carrara, one of the top provincial art museums in Italy.

14

16

15

16

15

Basic facts

Pavia, about 20 miles south of Milan on the banks of the River Ticino, was a former Ancient Roman colony and was at the heart of the Lombard Renaissance. In the 14th century it was incorporated into the state of Milan, ruled at the time by the Visconti family. From then on its

➡ Further afield

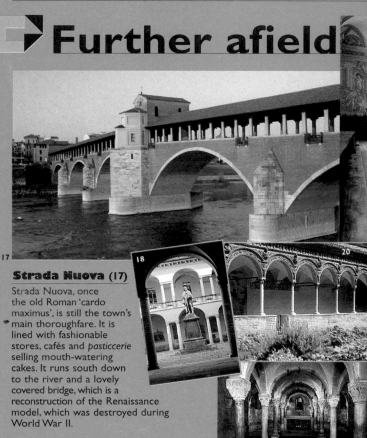

Strada Nuova (17)

Strada Nuova, once the old Roman 'cardo maximus', is still the town's main thoroughfare. It is lined with fashionable stores, cafés and *pasticcerie* selling mouth-watering cakes. It runs south down to the river and a lovely covered bridge, which is a reconstruction of the Renaissance model, which was destroyed during World War II.

Università (18)
Strada Nuova 65

The university's large Renaissance building was made considerably bigger at the end of the 18th century by Giuseppe Piermarini and Leopold Pollack. Just off one of the university's courtyards is the anatomy theater, designed by Pollack. At the top of the main staircase leading off the central courtyard is the physics theater, built in 1786 for the Como-born physicist, Alessandro Volta.

San Michele (19)
via Paolo Diacono ☎ 038226063

🔲 *open daily 7.30am–1pm, 2.30–7pm; public holidays 3–8pm* ● *admission free (donations welcome)*

This splendid Romanesque church is a reconstruction of an earlier Lombard church founded in 661. Its structure and somber interior have much in common with Milan's Sant'Ambrogio church ➡ 96. Frederico Barbarossa was crowned here in 1155.

history was inextricably linked to that of the Lombard capital. Pavia University is one of the oldest in Italy.

The Certosa's detailed decorative work is the origin of the expression, *lavoro certosino* ('painstaking work').

Certosa di Pavia (20)
☎ 0382925613

🕐 Tue.–Sun.; summer 9–11.30am, 2.30–6pm; winter 9–11.30am, 2.30–4.30pm; spring and autumn 9–11.30am, 2.30–5.30pm ● admission free

The Certosa, or charterhouse, a masterpiece of the Lombard Renaissance, is about six miles from Pavia on the north side of the vast grounds attached to Castello Visconteo. It was founded in 1396 by Gian Galeazzo Visconti, Duke of Milan, as a suitably grand setting for his family's tombs. The marble façade, designed by Giovanni Antonio Amadeo, is richly ornamented with statues, medallions and bas-reliefs. The interior is divided into three naves supported by large columns. The groined vaults are decorated with frescos by Ambrogio and Bernadino Bergognone.
★ In the left transept lie the tombs of Duke Ludovico il Moro and his wife, Beatrice d'Este, sculpted by Cristoforo Solari in the late 15th century.

Not forgetting

■ **Locanda Vecchia Pavia** via Cardinal Riboldi 2 ☎ 0382304132 🕐 Tue., Wed. eve.–Sun.; closed Jan. 1–10 *Classic Lombard cuisine.*
■ **Vecchio Mulino** piazzale Monumento 1, Certosa di Pavia ☎ 0382925894 🕐 Tue.–Sun. noon; closed Jan., Aug. *Traditional Lombard cuisine in a converted mill.*

Basic facts

Vigevano, southwest of Milan, is a hub of industrial activity and the capital of shoe manufacturing. The ruling families of Milan, the Visconti and then the Sforza, lived here and it is to them that the town owes a number of its monuments: the main square, one of the most beautiful

Further afield

Piazza Ducale (21)

Piazza Ducale, surrounded by arcades on three sides, was designed in 1492 by Bramante for Ludovico il Moro. It was built on the site of the medieval marketplace. Ludovico il Moro envisaged it as a sort of antechamber to the castle, and so it remained until the construction of a ramp linking the tower and the Visconti residence. It seems likely that Leonardo da Vinci was involved in the architectural design of the piazza, but the greater part of the actual work would have been carried out by local craftsmen, who built the vaults, arches, columns, the capitals and the medallions decorated with figures from Classical Antiquity, portraits of members of the Visconti family, and ancient proverbs. On the east side of the piazza can be seen the baroque façade of Sant'Ambrogio cathedral, begun in the 16th century and completed a century later.

Castello (22)
piazza Ducale ☎ 0381690370

🕐 Tue.–Sun. 8.30am–6pm; Mon. 2.30–6pm ● *admission free in the afternoons*
🕐 *Sun., public holidays 10am–6.30pm*

Concealed behind the colonnades of piazza Ducale is the castle, built in the 14th century for Luchino and Gian Galeazzo Visconti, and transformed into a sumptuous residence under Ludovico il Moro. The work was carried out by architect Donato Bramante, whose tower, visible from the piazza, still bears his name. Inside the complex there is the keep, *la loggia delle Dame* or hawk-house, the stables and the raised, covered road, over 160yds long, which linked the castle and the old fortress. The castle has been undergoing major renovation work in recent years.

Parco del Ticino (23)

The Ticino park straddles Piedmont and Lombardy. Cultivated fields alternate with woods, streams and heather. This idyllic setting is home to a number of protected species: weasels, wild boar, stone martens, badgers, hares and wild rabbits. There is an abundance of wild flowers, among them lilies, white and yellow water lilies and anemones. The numerous species of trees, some in danger of extinction, include beeches, acacias, white willows and Turkey oaks.

Not forgetting

■ **I Castagni** via Ottobiano 8/20 ☎ 038142860 🕐 Tue.–Sun. noon; closed Jan., Aug. *In a villa on the outskirts of the town you can sample the best cuisine in the Pavia region.*
■ **Antica Osteria del Ponte** piazza Negri 9, Cassinetta di Lugagnano ☎ 029420034 🕐 Tue.–Sat.; closed Christmas, Aug. *One of Italy's most famous restaurants serving fine cuisine in a typical Lombard house beautifully situated on the Naviglio Grande (the Grand Canal), on the road to Vigevano. Chef Ezio Santin's creations take their inspiration from the cuisine of Liguria and the Mediterranean.*

in Italy, and the castle, designed by Bramante.

Piazza Ducale is a splendid example of Renaissance architecture.

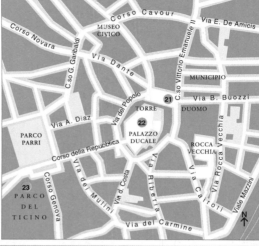

21

21

22

22

23

22

Where to shop

Seasons

The fashion designers are always one step ahead in Milan – store windows are filled with next season's styles. The winter sales start just after Christmas, the summer sales in the month of June.

Lunch-breaks

Traditionally, stores always opened from 9.30am to 12.30pm and from 3.30 to 7.30pm, closing on Monday mornings. However, large stores, fashion boutiques and most stores in the city center have changed their opening times so that they are more in keeping with other countries, and no longer close for lunch.

Supercentrale: open all year round!

Most Milanese leave the city during religious festivals and the month of August. When the whole of Milan seems closed and you can't find an open store or restaurant, make for the Supercentrale, open 365 days a year. It has bars, restaurants, a supermarket, a bookstore and stationer's, fax service…

entrances in piazza IV Novembre and Stazione Centrale ☎ 0266981277

75 Stores
THE INSIDER'S FAVORITES

From antiquity to the Middle Ages, the area surrounding the Duomo ➡ 86 was the hub of commerce and trade. Today luxury stores abound in the arcades, beneath the glass dome of Galleria Vittorio Emanuele II ➡ 86, and in the nearby streets. ■ Where to stay ➡ 18 ➡ 20

Where to shop

Grandi Magazizini Rinascente (1)
piazza del Duomo ☎ 0288521

M 1 Duomo; 3 Duomo **Department store** 🕒 Mon. 1–9pm, Tue.–Sat. 9am–9pm ☐ tax free, shipping 🍴 Bistrot Duomo ➡ 44 🍸 ⚑ viale Certosa 29 ☎ 023267051

Rinascente, the first Italian department store, opened in Milan in the 1920s, and has become a well-known commercial landmark. Giorgio Armani started off here as a window dresser. The store covers seven floors and has good ready-to-wear collections, perfumes and accessories. ★ On the top floor the store's restaurant has great views over the spires of the Duomo ➡ 86.

Libreria Internazionale Ulrico Hoepli (2)
via Hoepli 5 ☎ 02864871

M 1 Duomo; 3 Duomo **Books** 🕒 Mon. 2–7pm, Tue.–Sat. 9am–7pm ☐ shipping

The publisher Ulrico Hoepli specializes in technical books (covering everything from construction to floriculture). The bookstore is spread over six floors and is one of the city's biggest and best-stocked. There is a wide range of subject areas including literature, history, philosophy, technology and information technology. There are also foreign language books.

Ricordi Media Stores (3)
Galleria Vittorio Emanuele II ☎ 0286460272

M 1 Duomo; 3 Duomo **CDs, audio and video equipment, books, musical instruments and computer software** 🕒 Mon.–Sat. 9.30am–11.30pm; Sun. 10am–8pm ⚑ corso Buenos Aires 33 ☎ 0229526244 ☐ shipping

This multimedia paradise, covering two enormous floors in Milan's famous Galleria, used to be owned by Giuseppe Verdi's publisher. Today it serves as a haven for music lovers, bookworms, techies and video enthusiasts. The store also sells concert tickets and is equipped with an internet station for net surfers.

Borsalino (4)
Galleria Vittorio Emanuele II 92 ☎ 02874244 ➡ 0286450105

M 1 Duomo; 3 Duomo **Hats, accessories** 🕒 Mon. 11am–7.30, Tue.–Sat. 10am–7.30pm ☐ tax free, shipping ⚑ corso Vittorio Emanuele II 5 ☎ 02869 0805; via della Spiga 14 ☎ 0276022724

The borsalino, the wide-rimmed felt hat worn especially by men in the 1930s, is only one of many styles of hat (such as berets and panamas, among others) on sale here. Many other accessories are also available, including scarfs, gloves and belts for both men and women.

Not forgetting

■ **Savinelli (5)** via Orefici 2 ☎ 02876 660 Savinelli has been selling its own line in pipes, lighters and accessories for the smoker since 1876.

■ Where to eat ➥ 44
➥ 70 ■ After dark
➥ 78 ■ What to see
➥ 86 ➥ 88

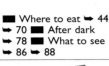

Borsalino

In the area

Elegant boutiques, movie theaters and bustling cafés nestle under the arcades of corso Vittorio Emanuele II. ■ Where to stay ➡ 18 ■ Where to eat ➡ 70

Where to shop

Fratelli Freni (6)
corso Vittorio Emanuele II 4 ☎ 02804871

Ⓜ *1 Duomo; 3 Duomo* **Cakes, ice creams** 🕐 *Mon., Wed.–Fri., Sun. 8.30am–midnight, Sat. 8.30–12.30am* ▤ ⑪ *via Torino 1 ☎ 02877072*

Fratelli Freni's small window is packed with an attractive, colorful display of charcuterie, sandwiches, and marzipan fruit and vegetables. ★ Other specialties include lemon and coffee flavored *granita* (iced drink) and jasmine ice cream.

Magli (7)
corso Vittorio Emanuele II/via San Paolo 1 ☎ 02865695

Ⓜ *1 Duomo; 3 Duomo* **Shoes** 🕐 *Mon. 3.30–8pm, Tue.–Sat. 10am–8pm* ▤ *tax free* ⑪ *via Manzoni 14 ☎ 02781264; via Orefici ☎ 028053719*

Magli, specialists in luxury shoes, stocks a huge range of elegant everyday shoes as well as evening and sports shoes for men and women.

Messaggerie Musicali (8)
Galleria del Corso 2 ☎ 0276055431

Ⓜ *1 Duomo; 3 Duomo* **CDs, videos, books, scores** 🕐 *Mon. 1–8.30pm, Tue.–Sun. 10am–11pm* ▤ *tax free*

This is the best music store in Milan. It stocks a vast selection of videos, books in Italian and foreign languages, and multimedia products.

United Colors of Benetton (9)
Galleria Passarella 1 ☎ 02794749

Ⓜ *1 San Babila* **Fashion, accessories** 🕐 *Mon. 2–7.30pm, Tue.–Sat. 10am–7.30pm* ▤ *tax free* ⑪ *corso Vittorio Emanuele II 9 ☎ 02795578 (children's clothes); piazza del Duomo 22 ☎ 02874307; via Dante 4 ☎ 028057404*

This large company, originally from Venice and famous worldwide for its colorful woolens and accessories, has opened its main store in Milan in piazza San Babila, selling ready-to-wear clothes for men, women and children. A wide range of accessories.

Fiorucci Dept. Store (10)
Galleria Passarella 1 ☎ 0276004896

Ⓜ *1 San Babila* **Sportswear, shoes, watches, bed and table linen, houseware** 🕐 *Mon. 3–7.30pm, Tue.–Sat. 10am–7.30pm* ▤ *tax free* 🅨

Casual ready-to-wear lines, designer fashion, as well as houseware, stationery and designer articles.

Not forgetting

■ **Ercolessi (11)** corso Vittorio Emanuele II 15 ☎ 0276000607 ⑪ corso Magenta 25 0286452444 *Pen store since 1921.*
■ **WP Store (12)** via Borgogna 3 ☎ 0276004694 *Casual clothing.*

Behind the Duomo is corso Vittorio Emanuele II, one of Milan's most elegant shopping streets.

Corso Vittorio Emanuele II opens onto piazza San Babila, which is also home to a number of stores. A network of cobbled streets, characteristic of old Milan, weaves its way around the piazza, and a short distance away is corso Venezia with its splendid neoclassical *palazzi*.

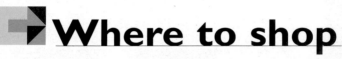 # Where to shop

Valextra (13)
piazza San Babila 1 ☎ 0276005024

M / San Babila **Leather goods** ◐ Mon. 3–7.30pm, Tue.–Sat. 10am–1.30pm, 3–7.30pm ☐ *tax free*

Since 1937 Valextra has been using high quality materials to create a range of luxury leather goods (travel bags, suitcases, purses, wallets, desk accessories). Influenced by Italian and international design, Valextra uses modern materials, such as plastic, and various kinds of leather, from the classic to the more unusual (elephant) for its goods.

Flos (14)
corso Monforte 9 ☎ 0276003639 ➡ 02780833

M / San Babila **Designer lamps** ◐ Mon. 3–7.30pm, Tue.–Sat. 9.30am–1pm, 3–7.30pm ☐

The 'Frisbi', a ceiling light made of tin, chrome, and steel wire, designed in 1978 by Achille Castiglione, is definitely the star of this collection of lighting fixtures. Stock includes innovatively designed lamps of all shapes and sizes. The lamps are by top designers including Philippe Starck, Pio Manzù, Pier Giacomo Castiglioni, Afra and Tobia Scarpa, and Marc Newson.

Boggi (15)
piazza San Babila 3 ☎ 0276000366

M / San Babila **Fashion and accessories** ◐ Mon. 3–7.30pm, Tue.–Sat. 10am–7.30pm ☐ *tax free* ▥ *via Dante 17 ☎ 02864 63562; largo Augusto 3 ☎ 02760 01489; corso di Porta Romana 76 ☎ 02583 14247; via Durini 28 ☎ 02760 05582 (womenswear)*

This chain of menswear stores favors the classic English look. Outfits for all occasions – businesswear, evening dress, casual clothes and sportswear. There is also a wide range of accessories.

Brigatti (16)
corso Venezia 15 ☎ 02760 00273

M / San Babila **Sportswear and equipment** ◐ Mon. 3–7.30pm, Tue.–Sat. 10am–1.30pm, 3–7.30pm ☐ *tax free, shipping*

Brigatti, occupying several floors of historic premises on corso Venezia, sells clothes and accessories for all kinds of sports, from the most common and popular to the more unusual (polo, hockey, curling…). The range includes classic sportswear for men and women: there are coats and loden jackets, and both English and American clothes for golfers.

Not forgetting

■ **De Padova (17)** corso Venezia 14 ☎ 02777201 *Furniture, couches, top Italian designer furniture.*

■ **Picowa (18)** Galleria San Babila 4/d ☎ 02794 078 *In a big three-story store; innovative designer furnishing.*

■ Where to eat ➡ 46

16
Whether for fashion, leather goods or accessories, Milan excels in elegance and quality.

16

15

15

13

13 17

14

14

In the area

Corso Matteotti, leading off piazza San Babila, is lined with fashionable shopping arcades. Not far away, in the middle of piazza Meda, stands *The Sun*, Arnaldo Pomodoro's famous statue. ■ Where to eat ➥ 44

Where to shop

Moroni Gomma (19)
corso Matteotti 14 ☎ 0276006821

Ⓜ *1 San Babila* **Rubber and plastic goods** 🕐 *Mon. 3–7pm, Tue.–Sat. 10am–7pm* 🔲 *tax free* 🚇 *via Niccolini 10 ☎ 02331 06565*

This elegant store has been selling rubber and plastic goods of all kinds since 1919. There is a large selection of plastic designer items, and a collection of sports clothing and casualwear.

Alessi (20)
corso Matteotti 9 ☎ 0276009062

Ⓜ *1 San Babila* **housewear** 🕐 *Mon. 3–7pm, Tue.–Sat. 10am–7pm* 🔲 *tax free*

This store stocks household accessories designed by top international designers such as Philippe Starck, Aldo Rossi, Ettore Sottsass, and Richard Sapper). There are original lemon-squeezers, cafetières, salt and pepper shakers in various materials (plastic, aluminum, and stainless steel) in a variety of colors.

Pomellato (21)
via San Pietro all'Orto/corso Matteotti ☎ 02783998

Ⓜ *1 San Babila* **Jewelry** 🕐 *Mon. 3–7pm, Tue.–Sat. 10am–7pm* 🔲 *tax free, shipping*

Pomellato's individual and distinctive style appeals to a wide international market. He designs jewelry and a wide variety of other items.

Richard-Ginori (22)
corso Matteotti 1/piazza Meda ☎ 0276002286

Ⓜ *1 San Babila* **Ceramics, china and glassware** 🕐 *Mon. 3.30–7.30pm, Tue.–Sat. 10am–7.30pm* 🔲 *tax free, shipping*

Milan's oldest and most prestigious manufacturer of china and ceramics. It stocks a large selection of its own dinner services as well as glassware and ceramics by other top manufacturers.

Jesurum (23)
via Verri 4 ☎ 0276015045

Ⓜ *1 San Babila* **Table linen and bedlinen** 🕐 *Mon. 3–7pm, Tue.–Sat. 10am–7pm* 🔲

A range of hand-finished napkins, sheets, bedspreads, towels and bathrobes. A top class store, one of Milan's oldest and most traditional.

Not forgetting

■ **Sant'Ambrœus (24)** corso Matteotti 7 ☎ 02760 00540 *Pastries, cakes, chocolate and panettone, a sweet, spiced bread made with candied fruit.*
■ **Frette (25)** via Monte Napoleone 21 ☎ 0276003791 *Linen and bedlinen as well as fine lingerie and underwear for the past 130 years.*

Via Verri
Piazza Meda
Via S. Paolo
Corso   Matteotti
Via S. Pietro all'Orto
Via Monte Napoleone
25 23 22 21 24 20 19
N

19

19

22

20

Alessi, established in Omegna (Piedmont) in 1921, is one of the world's best known Italian design names.

20

21

22

23

21

In the area

Exclusive via Monte Napoleone forms one side of the *quadrilatero d'oro* ('golden square') of Milan's fashion district (via della Spiga, via Sant'Andrea and via Borgospesso complete it). ■■ Where to stay ➡ 28 ■■ Where to eat ➡ 46 ■■ What to see ➡ 88

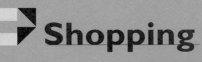

Shopping

26

26 26

Valentino (26)
via Monte Napoleone 20 ☎ 0276020285

Ⓜ *3 Montenapoleone* **Designer fashion** 🕐 *Mon. 3–7pm, Tue.–Sat. 10am–7pm* 🔲 *tax free, shipping* ◫ *via Santo Spirito 3* ☎ *0276006182*

On the corner of via Monte Napoleone and via Santo Spirito is the fashion boutique of the great Valentino Garavani. Garavani's creations cater for both the sophisticated, active, and feminine woman and the versatile, modern man. Valentino Garavani is the agent for a whole raft of labels, from the famous 'V' to 'Oliver', his range of everyday wear.

26

Gianni Versace (27)
via Monte Napoleone 11 ☎ 0276008528

Ⓜ *3 Montenapoleone* **Designer fashion and accessories** 🕐 *Mon. 3–7.30pm, Tue.–Sat. 10am–7.30pm* 🔲 *tax free, shipping* ◫ *via Monte Napoleone 2* ☎ *02760 01982-83*

Five floors of Versace menswear. On the third floor a large area is for womenswear. Accessories are available for both men and women.

Salvatore Ferragamo Uomo (28)
via Monte Napoleone 20/5 ☎ 0276006660

Ⓜ *3 Montenapoleone* **Accessories, shoes and designer fashion** 🕐 *Mon. 3–7pm, Tue.–Sat. 10am–7pm* 🔲 *tax free, shipping* ◫ *via Monte Napoleone 3* ☎ *0276000054 (women's fashion)*

Salvatore Ferragamo has provided exquisitely made shoes for a host of celebrities from Greta Garbo and Sophia Loren to Cecil B. de Mille. Salvatore Ferragamo also does a very successful line in accessories and ready-to-wear fashion and has recently opened a store selling womenswear next door.

■■ Where to shop
➡ 130

Via Monte Napoleone, nicknamed 'Montenapo', is Milan's smartest shopping street.

Venini (29)
via Monte Napoleone 9 ☎ 0276000539

Ⓜ 3 Montenapoleone **Glassware** 🕑 Mon. 2.30–7pm, Tue.–Sat. 10am–1.30pm, 3–7pm ▭ tax free, shipping

The island of Murano off the Venetian coast is world famous for its glass-making tradition and expertise. Venini is one of the most talented exponents of this school, producing blown glass – transparent or opaque – in a range of colors – vibrant or pale. Looking around his collection of vases, plates, boxes and other pieces has the feeling of being in an art gallery rather than in a store.

Not forgetting

■■ **Gucci (30)** via Monte Napoleone 5 and 27 ☎ 0276013050
The reputation of the Florentine label has traveled the world. Its flagship store in Milan sells its timeless classics: purses, belts, beautiful scarfs, shoes and its ready-to-wear collections for both men and women, all of them bearing the famous Gucci logo – two entwined 'G's.

In the area

Running perpendicular to via Monte Napoleone is via Sant'Andrea, a showcase for Milanese designer fashion, jewelry and accessories. On the corner of via della Spiga, providing that extra stylish touch, is a little stall selling rare flowers. ■ Where to stay ➡ 28 ■ Where to eat ➡ 46

◥ Where to shop

G. Lorenzi (31)
via Monte Napoleone 9 ☎ 0276022848 ➡ 76003390

Ⓜ *3 Montenapoleone* **Kitchenware, accessories** ◐ *Mon. 3–7.30pm, Tue.–Sat. 9am–12.30pm, 3–7.30pm* ▭

The ultimate kitchenware store, selling a whole range of utensils and cutlery, including highly ornate pieces and one-offs. ★ The store stocks pipes and accessories for the smoker and a variety of shaving accessories too. Customers can also visit the store's unusual little museum displaying shaving accessories.

Giorgio Armani (32)
via Sant'Andrea 9 ☎ 0276003234 ➡ 76014926

Ⓜ *3 Montenapoleone* **Ready-to-wear fashion** ◐ *Mon. 3–7.30pm, Tue.–Sat. 10am–7.30pm* ▭ *tax free, shipping* ▥ *via Durini 23 ☎ 02794248; via Durini 24 ☎ 0276003030; via Durini 25–7 ☎ 0276020306*

The divine Giorgio, pioneer of Milanese ready-to-wear fashion, directs his international fashion empire from his headquarters in via Borgonuovo. He is known for his modern and innovative style and his constant search for perfection.

35

GIORGIO ARMANI

32

32

31

31

At the Lorenzi museum, more than 2000 items illustrate the history of shaving.

31

31

■ What to see ➡ 88
■ Where to shop ➡ 128

Via A. Manzoni
Via Borgospesso
Via S. Spirito
Via Gesù
Via S. Andrea
Via Bagutta

29   27   11   34
            32   36
      8 11 35   12
M Montenapoleone
Via Monte Napoleone
M Montenapoleone   33   9
                                31

MISSONI

Missoni (33)
via Sant'Andrea/via Bagutta ☎ 02760 03555

M *3 Montenapoleone* **Designer fashion** 🕐 *Mon. 3–7pm, Tue.–Sat. 10am–7pm*
☐ *tax free*

Ottavio and Rosita Missoni make imaginative use of an extraordinary
range of colors; their designs feature squares, stripes, checks, waves and
patchwork rendered in a whole spectrum of shades. Their range of
leisure and evening wear uses a broad selection of textiles. Famous for
knitwear. There is a range of accessories to match the clothing.

Fendi (34)
via Sant'Andrea 6 ☎ 0276021617

M *3 Montenapoleone* **High-fashion accessories and fur** 🕐 *Mon. 3–7pm,
Tue.–Sat. 10am–7pm* ☐ *tax free, shipping*

Another big Italian name. The Fendi sisters, from Rome, have reached
new heights in fur fashion with their skillful tailoring. They have recently
launched a range of accessories designed with equal flair.

Not forgetting

■ **Trussardi (35)** via Sant'Andrea 5 ☎ 0276020380 🏠 piazza della Scala 5
☎ 028052054 *A big name in fashion, renowned for his sober, sporty lines.*
■ **Moschino (36)** via Sant'Andrea 12 ☎ 02760 00832
Shock-value designer fashion. Unmissable.

34   33

32   33

Via della Spiga, once a narrow little street in the shade of its rich neighbor, via Monte Napoleone, is now Milan's most famous thoroughfare and lined with exclusive boutiques. ▦ Where to stay ➡ 28 ➡ 29 ▦ Where to eat ➡ 46

➤ Where to shop

Gianfranco Ferré (37)
via della Spiga 11 ☎ 02794864

Ⓜ 3 Montenapoleone **Designer fashion** 🕐 Mon. 3–7pm, Tue.–Sat. 10am–1.30pm, 2.30–7pm ▣ tax free, shipping ⬆ via della Spiga 11/A (ready-to-wear for men) ☎ 02760 00385

Gianfranco Ferré's background in architecture is evident in his sophisticated creations, designed to flatter the female figure.

Krizia (38)
via della Spiga 23 ☎ 0276008429

Ⓜ 3 Montenapoleone **Designer fashion** 🕐 Mon. 3–7pm, Tue.–Sat. 10am–1.30pm, 2.30–7pm ▣ tax free, shipping

The eclectic grande dame of Italian fashion is famous for her animal motifs (especially tigers) and for the care with which she chooses her fabrics. The boutique on via Manin is the headquarters of the 'K' label and has a showroom and cultural space.

Prada (39)
via della Spiga 1 ☎ 0276008636

Ⓜ 1 San Babila **Shoes, leather goods, accessories, clothing** 🕐 Mon. 2.30–7pm, Tue.–Sat. 10am–7pm ▣ tax free, shipping ⬆ via Sant'Andrea 21 ☎ 02760 01426; galleria Vittorio Emanuele II 62–63 ☎ 02876 979; via Monte Napoleone 6 ☎ 0276020273

Krizia is associated with more than just fashion: her 'Spazio' on via Manin hosts a variety of cultural events.

A leather store known for the quality of its leather accessories (small leather goods, desk and travel accessories), its range of women's shoes and a large selection of other accessories in various materials. Prada has recently made an extraordinarily successful sortie into the world of street fashion. Although its ready-to-wear collection tends slightly toward the conservative – even austere – it is undeniably classy.

Tod's-Hogan (40)
via della Spiga 22 ☎ 0276002423

M 3 *Montenapoleone* **Shoes and sportswear** *Mon. 3–7pm, Tue.–Sat. 10am–7pm* ☐ *tax free*

Diego Della Valle, creator of Tod's and Hogan shoes and importer of Fay's jackets, has made a niche for himself on via della Spiga where he continues to impress his customers and the fashion world with his innovative and creative ideas. The secret of his success is the shoe (with its spiked anti-skid soles) described as casual, but which is elegant enough to be worn with the smartest suit. For special occasions, Tod's come in patent leather.

Not forgetting

■ **L'utile e il dilettevole (41)** via della Spiga 46 ☎ 0276008420
Furniture, accessories and linen from all over Europe. Full of attractive and useful items for the home as well as lots of gift ideas, which may be less practical but are likely to be more fun.

In the area

The lively, pedestrianized area covering via Fiori Chiari, via Madonnina and the maze of adjoining streets is full of unusual boutiques, and cafés and restaurants with charming terraces. ■ Where to eat ➡ 48 ■ After dark ➡ 78 ➡ 82 ■ What to see ➡ 99

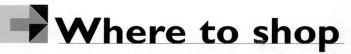

Where to shop

MGB Maria Grazia Baldan (42)
via Tivoli 6 ☎ 0286463559

Ⓜ 2 Lanza **Jewelry** 🕐 Mon. 2.30–7pm, Tue.–Sat. 10am–1pm, 2.30–7pm 🖃 tax free, shipping

Maria Grazia Baldan draws upon many different cultures for inspiration. The lovingly restored elegant *palazzo* which houses her boutique is a perfect showcase for her collection of jewelry and ornaments.

Diego Dalla Palma (43)
via Madonnina 13–15 ☎ 02876818

Ⓜ 2 Lanza **Beauty products, cosmetics** 🕐 Mon. 3.30–7.30pm, Tue.–Sat. 10am–7.30pm 🖃 ☷ via Agnello 19 ☎ 02874 080

A famous hairstylist, Diego Dalla Palma, sells a range of cosmetics from his store in the heart of Brera and also shows clients the art of applying make-up.

Decomania (44)
via Fiori Chiari 7 ☎ 0286463413

Ⓜ 2 Lanza **Art deco work and jewelry** 🕐 Mon. 3.30–7pm, Tue.–Sat. 10am–1pm, 3.30–7pm 🖃 tax free, shipping

Gianfranco Ceccarini is an avid collector of art deco pieces and furniture. His quaint little boutique stocks exquisite jewelry and other valuable items.

Etro (45)
via Pontaccio/vicolo Fiori ☎ 02864 61192

Ⓜ 2 Lanza **Fabrics, clothing, leather goods, perfume** 🕐 Mon. 3–7pm, Tue.–Sat. 10am–2pm, 3–7pm 🖃 tax free, shipping ☷ via Monte Napoleone 5 ☎ 0276005049; via Verri/via Bigli ☎ 0276005450

This store stocks sophisticated fabrics for creating a stylish outfit or for designing a romantic interior. There are luxury cashmeres, refined and elegant clothes, attractive leather accessories and a wide collection of perfumes, as well as a selection of unusual and beautiful bottles.

Torriani (46)
via Mercato 5 ☎ 02866519

Ⓜ 2 Lanza **Masks and costumes** 🕐 Mon. 3–6.45pm, Tue.–Sat. 9.30am–12.30pm, 3–6.45pm 🖃

Signor Torriani is always happy to give customers advice on party surprises, and will even demonstrate his stock of jokes and tricks, and show you his gruesome Halloween selection.

Not forgetting

■ **L'Oro dei Farlocchi (47)** via Madonnina 5 ☎ 02860589 *Antiques and unusual pieces.*

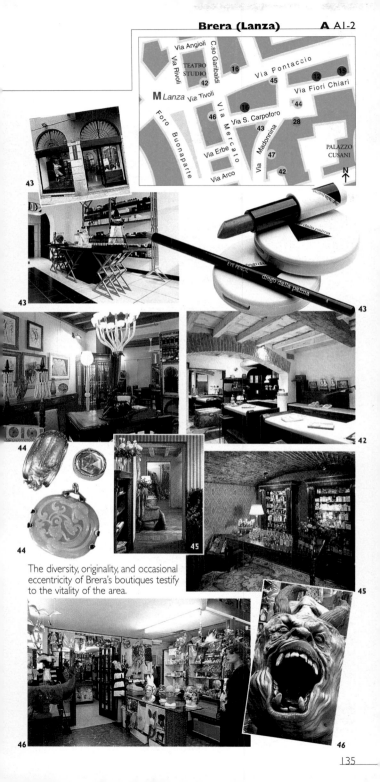

The diversity, originality, and occasional eccentricity of Brera's boutiques testify to the vitality of the area.

Where to shop

Merù (48)
via Solferino 3 ☎ 0286460700

Ⓜ 2 Lanza **Jewelry** 🕐 Mon. 3.30–7pm, Tue.–Sat. 9.30am–1pm, 3.30–7.30pm ▭

An assorted collection of jewelry and small ornamental objects imported from the Mereu brothers' native Sardinia. Ranging from simple gold and enamel pieces to more elaborately crafted work and even some antique finds, the selection has an extremely broad appeal. At the back of the small store there is a workshop where the Mereu brothers design their own jewelry. They will be pleased to show you the work in progress, and will also accept commissions.

Penelopi 3 (49)
via Solferino/via Ancona ☎ 026599640

Ⓜ 2 Lanza **Houseware** 🕐 Mon. 3–7.30pm, Tue.–Fri. 10am–2pm, 3–7.30pm; Sat. 10am–1pm, 3–7.30pm ▭ tax free

Penelopi 3, which is located by the side of the church of San Marco ➥ 100, is a store where you will find everything from wastepaper baskets to kitchen utensils. It is crammed with a huge selection of multicolored items in a bewildering variety of materials, both natural and artificial. The range includes not only innovative work made in Italy but also more exotic articles from Africa, Asia, America and the rest of Europe.

La Porcellana Bianca (50)
via Statuto 11 ☎ 026571560

Ⓜ 2 Moscova **China, ceramics, houseware** 🕐 Mon. 3–7pm, Tue.–Sat. 10am–2pm, 3–7pm ▭ tax free 🚌 viale Piave 29 ☎ 0276015701

This boutique is a hymn to the color white. There are plates, dishes, jugs, tea and coffee cups, carafes, tureens – and everything is white or off-white. The store also stocks glassware, stainless steel kitchen utensils, and an assortment of aprons and tea cloths in a variety of colors. It also stocks a fun selection of different tea cozies.

Mirabello (51)
via Montebello/via San Marco ☎ 02654887

Ⓜ 2 Moscova **Furnishing fabrics, bedlinen** 🕐 Mon. 3–7pm, Tue.–Sat. 10am–1pm, 3–7pm ▭ tax free 🚌 **Mirabello In** via Montebello/largo Treves ☎ 026555629

This store has a wide selection of beautiful luxury furnishing fabrics, wallpaper, drapes, table linen and bedlinen. ★ You can choose from many colors and styles and can even have your purchases embroidered with your own monogram.

Not forgetting

■ **Rossignoli (52)** corso Garibaldi 71 ☎ 02804960 🚌 corso Garibaldi 65 ☎ 0286460295 *Touring and leisure bicycles as well as hybrid and mountain bikes for men, women and children, in addition to cycling accessories.*

dark ➡ 78 ■ What
to see ➡ 100

Purple pansies, cute pandas, golden
cherubs… all found on Merù's
pendants.

In the area

Corso Garibaldi opens onto piazza Porta Garibaldi, once part of the wall that surrounded the city in the 17th century. Boutiques, bars, restaurants and dance clubs abound in this lively area. ■ Where to eat ➡ 56 ➡ 66 ➡ 68 ■ After dark ➡ 76 ➡ 78 ➡ 80

Where to shop

Cotti (53)
via Solferino 42 ☎ 0229001096

Ⓜ 2 Moscova **Wine** Ⓞ *Tue.–Sat. 8am–1pm, 3–7.30pm* ▣ *shipping*

Luigi Cotti has been selling high-quality wines and liqueurs from the Italian peninsula and from around the world since 1952. His cellar, which is maintained at just the right temperature, is stocked with more than 1300 wines. Cotti also sells a range of sweet and savory gourmet items, which will make tasty accompaniments to your chosen beverage. Dozens of varieties of grappa and whiskey offer further temptation.

High-Tech (54)
piazza XXV Aprile 12 ☎ 026241101

Ⓜ 2 Garibaldi F.S. **Furniture, houseware, kitchen utensils** Ⓞ *Tue.–Sun. 10.30am–7.30pm* ▣ *tax free, shipping*

The architect Mauro Bacchini, who began in business importing stainless steel furniture and accessories from the United States in the 1970s, decided to expand his main store in Porta Garibaldi to include a wider range of products for the household and family. Today this immense Aladdin's cave contains furniture, clothes, kitchen equipment, tableware, lamps and gadgets. Many of the items are amazingly original and all are of the highest quality.

10 Corso Como (55)
corso Como 10 ☎ 0229002674

Ⓜ 2 Garibaldi F.S. **Clothing, jewelry and exotic artwork** Ⓞ *Mon. 3.30–7.30pm, Tues., Thur.–Sun., 10.30am–7.30pm, Wed. 10.30am–9pm* ▣ *tax free, shipping* ⊞

Carla Sozzani, a woman with eclectic tastes, is constantly in search of the exotic. Fascinated by Eastern cultures, she has transformed her store on corso Como into a sort of bazaar stocked with objects of all descriptions: glassware from Murano, Moroccan tableware, lamps, men's and women's clothing, ethnic jewelry and much more. There is a gallery space and a bookstore on the second floor.

Il Telefono (56)
viale Pasubio 8 ☎ 0229006594

Ⓜ 2 Garibaldi F.S. **Mobile phones and accessories** Ⓞ *Mon. 3.15–7.30pm, Tue.–Sat. 9.15am–1pm, 3.15–7.30pm* ▣ *tax free*

This unusual store carries a huge array of mobile phones from second-hand models to the very latest designs. There are also cordless phones, answering machines, old-fashioned telephones and accessories. All at reasonable prices.

Not forgetting

■ **Movo (57)** piazza Principessa Clotilde 8 ☎ 026554836 *Everything for the model enthusiast – airplanes, trains, cars, boats, tin soldiers...*

The streets in this area converge on Porta Garibaldi, once part of the walls that used to surround the city.

Where to shop

Bardelli (58)
corso Magenta 13 ☎ 0286450734

Ⓜ / Cairoli **Classic clothing** 🕐 Mon. 3–7.30pm, Tue.–Sat. 10am–7.30pm
▤ tax free, shipping 🚇 via Madonnina 19–21 ☎ 028057426

Over the years the Bardelli boutique has steadily expanded and it now covers several floors. It has established itself as one of Milan's top ready-to-wear stores. Quality fabrics such as cashmere, worsted wool, linen, and cotton are used to create garments for men and women that are very much in the classic English style. The store also stocks a good range of attractive accessories that designed to complement the clothing.

Buscemi (59)
corso Magenta 31 ☎ 02804103

Ⓜ / Cadorna **Records, CDs, cassettes** 🕐 Mon. 3–7.30, Tue.–Sat. 9am–1.30pm, 3–7.30pm

Buscemi, opposite bar Magenta ➡ 78, one of Milan's oldest bars, has a good stock of pop, rock and jazz music, ranging from the established classics of each genre to the latest releases. Next door, Buscemi Classica boasts a fine selection of classical music, including rare recordings.

Marchesi (60)
via Santa Maria alla Porta 11a ☎ 02876730

Ⓜ / Cairoli **Cakes and confectionery** 🕐 Tue.–Sat. 7.30am–8pm, Sun. 8.30am–1pm ▤ ▥

Marchesi was established at the end of the 19th century by the grandfather of the present owner and still occupies the same premises. A large assortment of candy, pralines, petit fours is on offer. The popular Milanese specialty, *panettone* (a sweet, spicy bread containing candied fruit) is also served and sold here. ★ Breakfasts and aperitifs are served at the counter.

Galleria Blanchaert (61)
via Nirone 19 ☎ 0286451700

Ⓜ / Cadorna **Antiques, objets d'art** 🕐 Tue.–Sat. 10am–1pm, 4–7.30pm ▤

Jean Blanchaert, has been an antique dealer in Milan for the past 40 years. This store has a wonderful selection of Murano glassware (1700–1950), Biedermeier and Charles X pieces, as well as a range of contemporary designs. ★ Close to the Sant'Ambrogio basilica ➡ 96 Galleria Blanchaert regularly organizes temporary exhibitions.

Not forgetting

■ **Casati (62)** via Carducci 9 ☎ 0286452009 *Established in the 19th century, this winestore stocks some 2000 wines and spirits.*
■ **Città del Sole (63)** via Orefici 13 ☎ 0286461683 *Educational and ecological toys.*

STAZIONE
FERROVIE
NORD
MILANO
M *Cadorna*
Piazza Castello
M *Cairoli*
Via Cusani
Piazzale
Cadorna
Largo
Cairoli
Foro Buonaparte
TEATRO
DAL VERME
Via Puccini
Via Illica
Via Carducci
62
Via S.Nicolao
35
Corso
59
12
Magenta
Via S. Giovanni sul Muro
Via Porlezza
Via Campero
Via Dante
Via Rovello
Via Broletto
23
24
Via Meravigli
M *Cordusio*
Piazza
Cordusio
Via Oreuci
Via S.M. alla Porta
BORSA
Via Negri
36 25
58
3
60
Largo
Anspero
Piazza
d. Affari
63
61
Via S. Agnese
Via Nirone
Via Luini
N

63

59

58

61

Wine, mouth-watering delicacies,
gadgets, music, clothing and accessories
– all available in one district.

60

60

In the area

The area around the city's former docks is still characteristic of old Milan. It has been colonized by artists and antique dealers, and bars and restaurants have multiplied and attract ever-increasing numbers.
■ Where to eat ➡ 62 ■ After dark ➡ 82 ■ What to see ➡ 94

Where to shop

Cavalli e Nastri (64)
corso di Porta Ticinese 46 ☎ 0289409452

⊞ 15 *Vintage clothing and jewelry* ◕ Mon. 3.30–7.30pm, Tue.–Sat. 9.30am–12.30pm, 3.30–7.30pm ▱ shipping

Elegance is the theme here, whether it's day or evening wear, for men or for women. The clothes are all retro fashion styles, and range in date from the 1920s through to the 1960s. The fascinatingly diverse stock includes American, English, French and, of course, Italian designs. This store is an absolute must for lovers of retro fashion. The store also sells a very up-market range of vintage accessories and highly sophisticated antique jewelry.

Dock of the bay (65)
viale Gorizia 30 ☎ 0258100034

⊞ 9, 47, 59, 74 *Casual clothing* ◕ Mon. 3.30–7.30, Tue.–Sat. 9.30am–1pm, 3.30–7.30pm ▱ shipping

Dock of the bay occupies two adjoining stores, (one for men, one for women), overlooking the Darsena, Milan's old docks ➡ 94. The prevailing look here is hip and modern. There are deep colors and simple fluid lines for men, and bright colors or delicate shades with a more tailored line for women.

Il Discomane (66)
alzaia Naviglio Grande 38 ☎ 028394860

⊞ 13, 15 *Second-hand records* ◕ Mon. 3.30–7pm, Tue.–Sat. 9.30am–1pm, 3.30–7pm ▱ shipping

The store's collection of old 78s and 45s will delight vinyl enthusiasts. All types of music are stocked, though there is a particularly fine selection of jazz and classical music. The store also stocks a number of rare items that will attract and appeal to collectors.

Studio d'arte Alfredo Pieramati (67)
alzaia Naviglio Grande 4 ☎ 028357361

⊞ 2 *Paintings, lithographs, reproductions* ◕ Tue.–Sat. 10am–noon, 3–7pm ▱

Alfredo Pieramati is the much-loved painter-poet of old Milan; his paintbrush brings the old tenement blocks and working-class quarters to life. In many cases his canvases are the only remaining record of picturesque spots that have now disappeared. His best-known views, widely reproduced, are of the canals and Brera.

Not forgetting

■ **Punti di vista (68)** ripa di Porta Ticinese 55 ☎ 0289404277 *Gadgets, collectable items.* Ⓜ *corso Buenos Aires 75 ☎ 026692621*
■ **Libreria Pontremoli (69)** via Vigevano 15 ☎ 0258103806 *Antiquarian books, prints, rare editions.*

IL TRIONFO
DEL
TRESSETTE
POEMA EROICO-GIOCOSO
PER
PATRIZIO VENETO.

IN VINEGIA

69

DOCK
OF THE BAY

NAVIGLIO GRANDE

STUDIO A. PIERAMATI

Basic facts

Markets are set up twice a week in each district of Milan. Fruit, vegetable, meat and fish stalls tend to predominate, but there is also a fair number of clothing and shoe stalls. The weekend collectors' markets will delight bargain-hunters and antique-lovers.

Where to shop

Mercato di viale Papiniano (70)
viale Papiniano

🅼 2 Sant'Agostino *Fruit, vegetables, clothes, shoes, flowers* 🕒 *Tue. am, Sat.*

This is the city's largest market. There is a cheerful, bustling atmosphere on Tuesdays and even more so on Saturdays when the stallholders take over the whole length of viale Papiniano. ★ As you browse through the stalls you might just be lucky enough to pick up a bargain here, especially at the stalls selling designer seconds.

Fiera di Senigallia (71)
viale D'Annunzio – Darsena

▣ 3, 15 *Accessories, utensils, bric-a-brac, second-hand goods* 🕒 *Sat.*

The Senigallia flea market is held in a quiet pedestrianized area on the banks of the Darsena ➡ 94, and is perhaps the most characteristic of all Milan's markets. It is worth having a good look around as a wide variety of goods are to be found here and some stalls sell anything and everything. ★ Rummage through the second-hand book and record stalls where you may well find some rarities and bargains.

Mercatone dell'antiquariato (72)
ripa di Porta Ticinese

▣ 47 *Antiques, furniture, vintage clothing* 🕒 *last Sun. of the month*

Antique dealers and collectors gather along the banks of the Naviglio Grande (Grand Canal) on the last Sunday of each month. There are often rare and sometimes exceptional items to be found here, although you should not expect bargains. Many of these dealers are also the owners of more permanent and well-established concerns and know the full value of the items they are selling. But if you're after something special, do make time to visit this fine market. The picturesque setting alone makes it worthwhile.

Mercatino di via Brembo (73)
via Brembo–via Lorenzini

🅼 3 Lodi Tibb *Antiquarian books, furniture, bric-a-brac* 🕒 *Sun. am*

This is where the real bargain hunters come; as Senigallia moved further upmarket, many second-hand goods and clothes dealers went elsewhere and many of them gravitated toward this rail depot at Porta Romana. Bargains are certainly there to be found, although finding them may require patience and perseverance.

Not forgetting

▪ **Mercato filatelico (74)** via Armorari 🕒 Sun. am *A stamp-collectors' market. Also postcards and coins.*
▪ **Mercato dei fiori (75)** piazzetta Reale 🕒 Mar.–June and Oct.–Nov. Sun. am *A wide selection of house plants, outdoor plants and flowers at reasonable prices.*

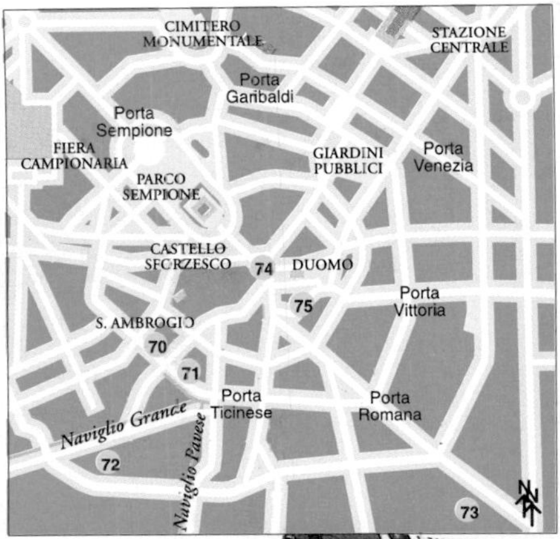
CIMITERO MONUMENTALE
STAZIONE CENTRALE
Porta Garibaldi
Porta Sempione
FIERA CAMPIONARIA
PARCO SEMPIONE
GIARDINI PUBBLICI
Porta Venezia
CASTELLO SFORZESCO
74
DUOMO
75
Porta Vittoria
S. AMBROGIO
70
71
Porta Ticinese
Porta Romana
Naviglio Grande
72
Naviglio Pavese
73
N

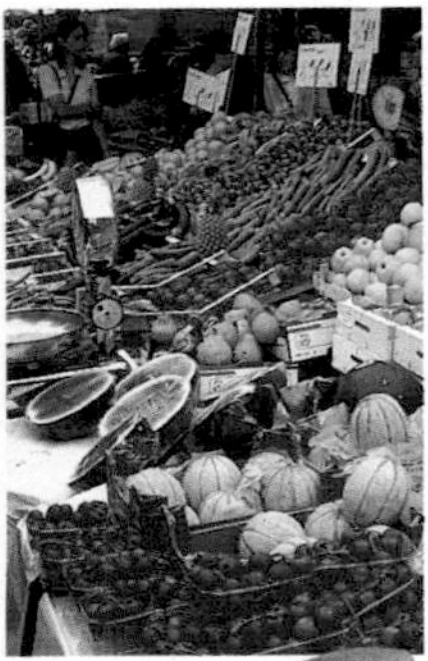
70

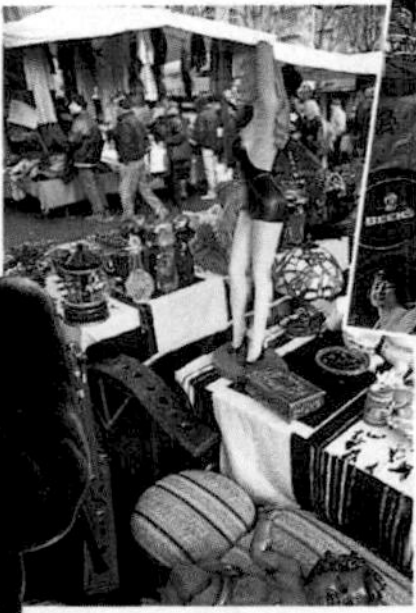
71

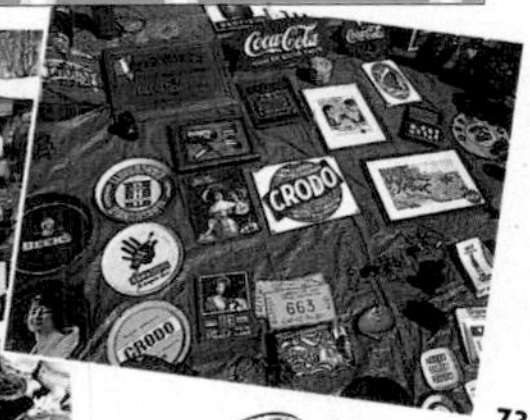
CRODO
CRODO
73

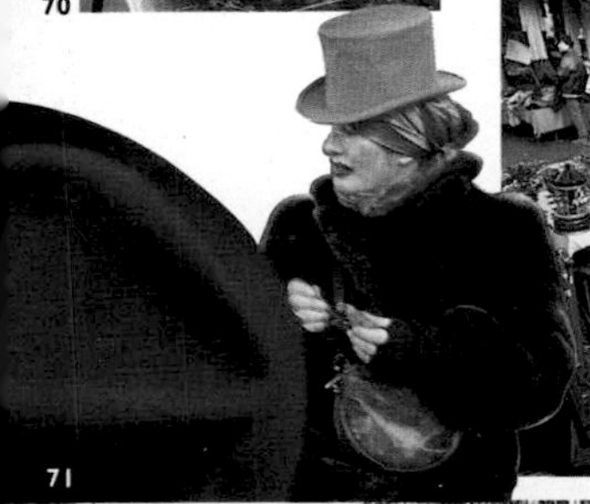
71

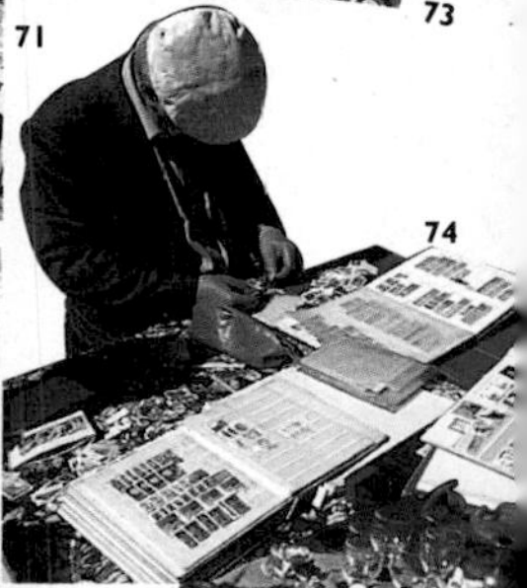
74

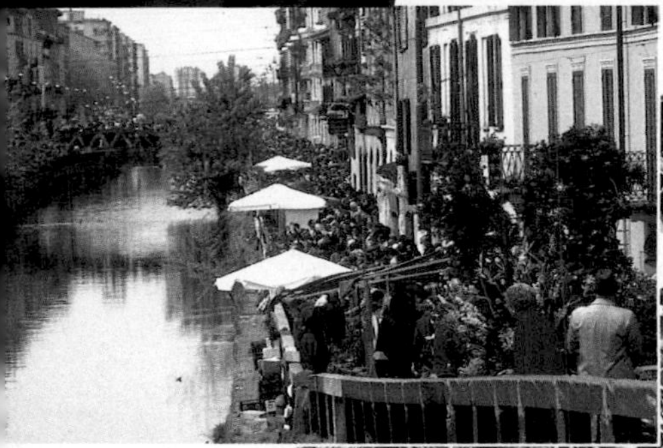
72

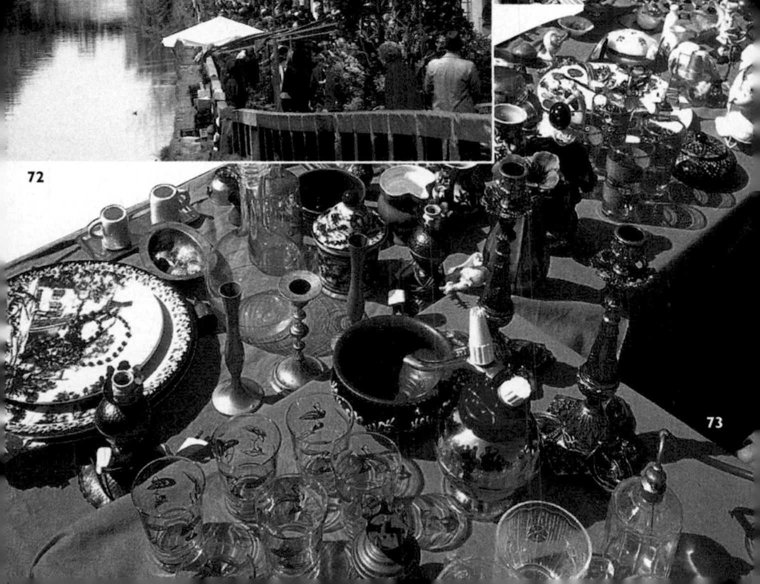
73

→ Finding your way

The police
The *Vigili Urbani* (urban police) are responsible for directing traffic when there are traffic jams or accidents. They also make good guides and are usually able to give you directions if you lose your way.

MONTENAPOLEON

Milan, a city within rings

Milan has two boundary rings around it (today marked by beltways): the innermost ring surrounds the medieval core of the city and connects Castello Sforzesco to the old city gates (clockwise: Magenta, Sempione, Volta, Garibaldi, Nuova, Venezia, Monforte, Vittoria, Romana, Vigentina, Lodovica, Ticinese and Genova); the outer ring corresponds to the extension of the city limits during the Renaissance.

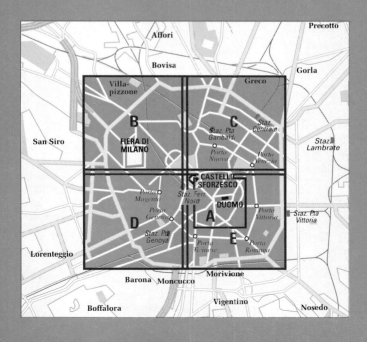

For each street, the letter in bold refers to one of the maps (**A–E**), and the letters and numbers mark the corresponding square in which it is found.

Index
of streets

Subway map

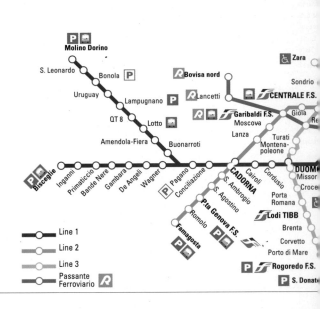

Molino Dorino
S. Leonardo
Bonola
Uruguay
Lampugnano
QT 8
Lotto
Amendola-Fiera
Buonarroti
Bisceglie
Inganni
Primaticcio
Bande Nere
Gambara
De Angeli
Wagner
Pagano
Conciliazione
Famagosta
Romolo
Pta Genova F.S.
S. Agostino
S. Ambrogio
CADORNA
Cairoli
Cordusio
DUOMO
Missori
Croce
Porta Romana
Lodi TIBB
Brenta
Corvetto
Porta di Mare
Rogoredo F.S.
S. Donato
Bovisa nord
Lancetti
CENTRALE F.S.
Garibaldi F.S.
Moscova
Lanza
Turati
Montenapoleone
Zara
Sondrio
Gioia
Re

Line 1
Line 2
Line 3
Passante Ferroviario

Abbreviations

c.so = corso (avenue) p.le = piazzale (large sq.) v. = via (road)
l.go = largo (small square) p.za = piazza (square) v.le = viale (boulevard)

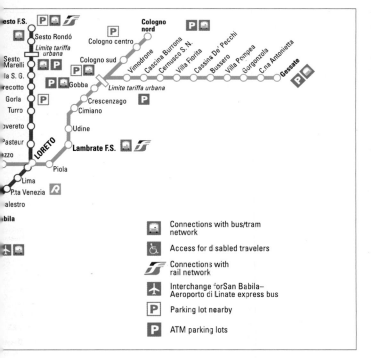

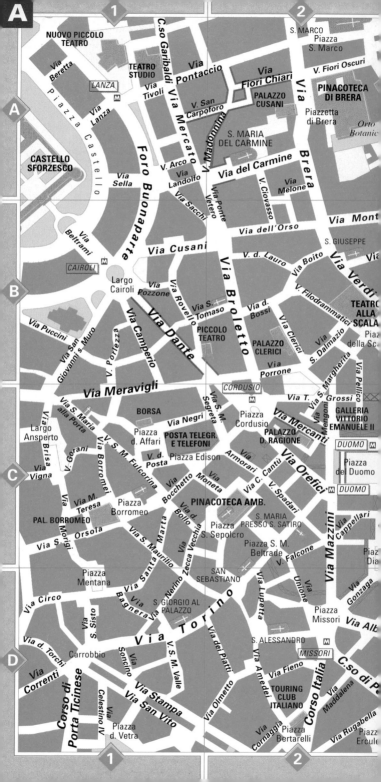

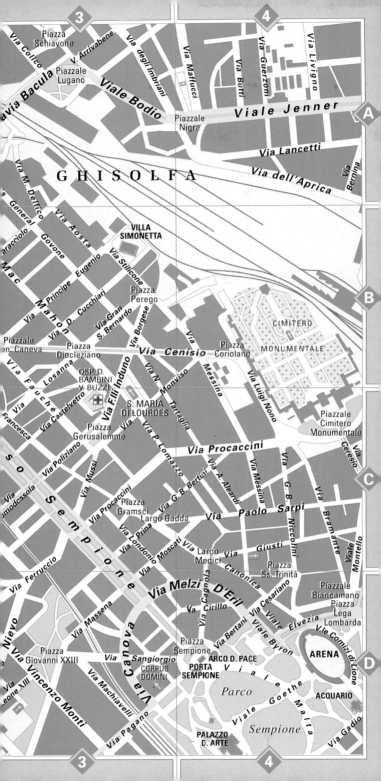

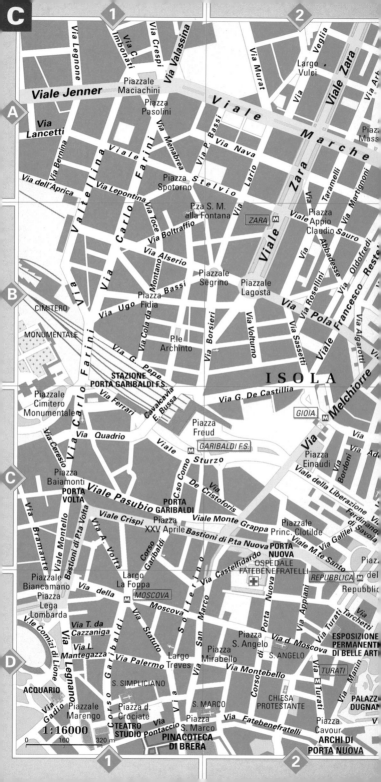

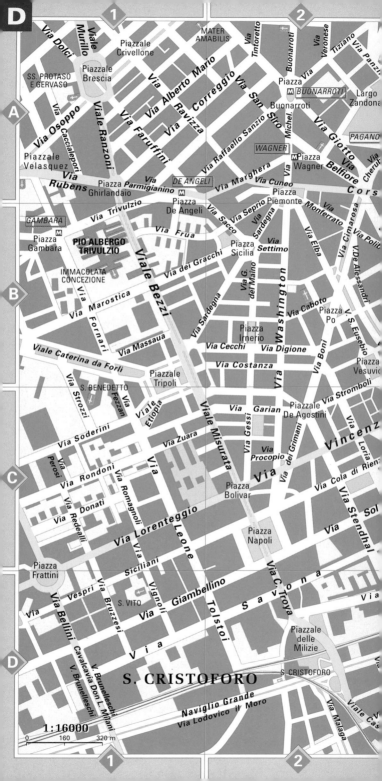

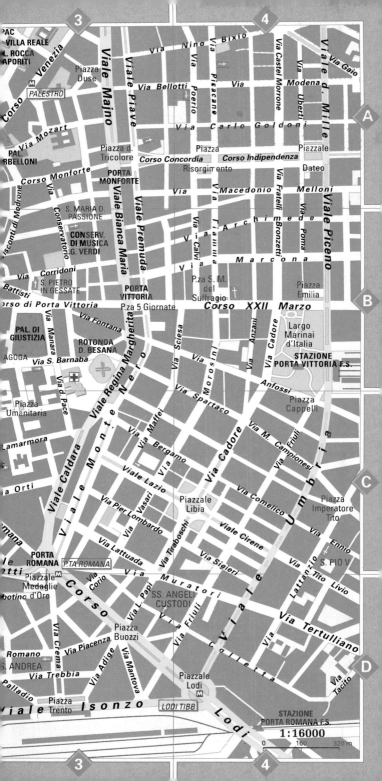

General index

Practical information and advice on traveling to Milan and finding your way around the city is given on pages 6 to 15.

Index